Three Cars in Every Garage

By Richard R. Mathison

The Eternal Search
God Is a Millionaire

PLATE *1   The Automobile Club of Southern California headquarters at Adams and Figueroa opened in 1923.*

Three Cars in Every Garage

A Motorist's History of the Automobile and the Automobile Club in Southern California

RICHARD R. MATHISON

50320

DOUBLEDAY & COMPANY, INC., GARDEN CITY, NEW YORK

1968

Acknowledgments

While many people were helpful in collecting historical material for this volume, particular thanks should be given to Joseph E. Havenner, Harry V. Cheshire, Jr., J. Allen Davis, Patrice Manahan, Larry Meyer and Floyd Clymer.

R.R.M.

CONTENTS

CONTENTS

Three Cars in Every Garage

Chapter 1

THE RICH MAN'S TOY

Motoring is a stimulating and rather dangerous amusement. When not overdone, it is healthful and pleasant. Ladies should wear warm, wool garments free from encumbering draperies with heavy shoes and sensible gloves. Her escort should provide a protective duster and goggles. No young lady should go alone with a gentleman on an extended afternoon motoring trip. An automobile often stops without apparent cause and is sometimes in disrepair for hours or even all night. A party composed entirely of young people should have a chaperon.

—Etiquette of Social and Official Life with Superb, Descriptive and Picturesque Illustrations, 1901.

History may not be "bunk," as Henry Ford once called it. But it has an unhappy facility of recording for posterity the dreariest of statistics while the merriest picnics are forgotten; it forgets jolly banter and quip while it carefully recalls the dullest of political pomposities.

Hence, one can only look at the ten brave men who founded the Auto Club of Southern California through the dim mirror of time and apply James Bondian deduction.

They must have been adventurous young blades, or they would not have been so daring as to flaunt the newfangled contraption before their more sedate peers. From records of the time, they must also have been a bit dashing and cavalier, perhaps not averse to buzzing by a neurotic drayhorse at a breakneck eight miles per hour just for the sheer joy of it. They must have loved the sporting life, for their annals are studded with concern over races and contests. They must have been gentlemen of reasonable income, for an automobile was no toy for a payday workman. And, above all, they must have felt themselves, if not far-seeing pioneers, a persecuted minority in a world of stuffy buggy-lovers and cautious stick-in-the-muds.

The bold ten who first assembled were: Russell D. Holabird, John H. Martindale, Harry C. Turner, Homer Laughlin, Walter D. Wise, Lee Chamberlain, William K. Cowan, William Lambert, Edward T. Off and Arthur L. Hawes.

Six were present that December 13, 1900, the day when both the articles were filed and the first officers were elected. Chamberlain was elected president; Wise, vice president; Holabird, secretary; and Turner was made treasurer. They decided to meet three days later. But, on December 16, not enough showed up for a quorum. It was April, 1903, more than two years later, before another meeting was called.

Their articles of incorporation have the subtle flavor of men on the defensive. The non-profit association, they explained, was for all persons who owned or were interested in self-propelled vehicles. They went on to declare themselves ready to promote favorable legislation for such vehicles, as well as good roads for their use, and to "protect the lawful rights and privileges" of all auto owners.

One can only view with amusement, mingled with awe, the "rich man's toy" of that day. Typical was the Porter Stanhope, priced at $750, weighing in at 550 pounds. Its creator in Boston boasted it was "a handsome stylish vehicle which can be started instantly and without previous laborious and lengthy preparation." It could be stopped instantly and could run "at any speed up to twenty-five miles per hour." The vehicle, early ads claimed, had "none of the inherent faults of the horse and no new ones of its own at the present time." In appearance, in fact, it exactly resembled a "horseless carriage." Still others were available for those few enthusiasts who could afford such luxuries. The first White Steamer was made in Cleveland in 1900, and the Phelps Tractor of 1901 was a steam-propelled, large vehicle which could go twenty miles an hour. The Oldsmobile, Spiner, Winton were on the market and the California Automobile Company of San Francisco produced a "stylish, little runabout" which cost only $500. Others, steam cars ("no smell, no noise, no jolt"), water-gasoline, cars on tracks, were just over the horizons.

To fully appreciate the pioneering implications of our brave little band of gentlemen, one must look briefly at the time when they started their association.

In distant Detroit, a thousand whistle stops across the U.S., Henry Ford, chief engineer at the Detroit Edison Company, who'd built his first auto just seven years before, was perfecting his newfangled gasoline engine. Supposedly, the gruff wizard, Thomas Edison, had set him on his course in 1896 when he'd told young Ford to stick to gasoline as a source of power. "Electric cars must keep near to power plants," Edison had reportedly said. "The storage battery is too heavy. Steam cars . . . have to have a boiler and fire. You have the thing! Keep to it!" Ford did—and so set the pattern for the great U.S. industry to come. But it was to be nearly a decade before this visionary's dream of a light, mass-produced automobile was to be a reality. While the first gasoline engine itself, credited to Daimler, had been built in 1884, it was actually a culmination of an idea which reached back some 250 years, when the concept of using power generated by the explosion of gunpowder to move vehicles was first suggested. From this basic idea hundreds of internal combustion designs were devised using gas (not gasoline), steam, crude oil, electricity and nearly anything which could burn, sputter or pop.

Americans faced this new century with an optimism which bordered on arrogance. The last century had been marked by scientific progress which the New York *Times* noted in 1899 "relegated all the science that preceded . . . to the same category as the lore of the Chaldeans and the Egyptians." Prosperity was back. The Klondike had brought in a new flow of gold. International exchange ran to U.S. advantage, and President McKinley put the U.S. on the gold standard in 1900. Progress was everywhere. Business mergers had numbered 1208 in 1899 as compared with 303 the year before. The mighty U. S. Steel Corporation was born in 1901 when Andrew Carnegie agreed to sell out for $492 million and J. Pierpont Morgan agreed to help finance the merger of twelve of the greatest steel companies. With this consolidation would come a pressing need to find new markets for steel, which subtly hastened the auto's emergence.

One local consolidation was already at work in southern California. Union Oil Co. of California had been organized in 1890 in Santa Paula. Edward L. Doheny and Charles A. Canfield had dug their first oil well with a pick and shovel in a city lot near the present corner of Second Street and Glendale Boulevard in 1892. Several hundred similar enterprising entrepreneurs had small wells going in the city and more were exploring the Kern River and Coalinga area.

The economy was poised and ready to absorb such a massive new industry as auto manufacturing. By 1900 only four out of ten workers were still in agriculture; the growing trend was for more and more people to move to the city—where the auto would have its first major impact. The U.S. was already the leading industrial country in the world. Still, labor and resultant purchasing power had not yet caught up with the tide. The average workweek was fifty-nine hours and the average unskilled worker's weekly paycheck was $10—hardly a mass market for the "rich man's toy." But the trend toward more leisure and an affluent middle class was obvious.

The jiggling and belching automobile was appearing more frequently on city streets, though it was still an oddity in the backlands. In 1900 a total of 4,192 autos were manufactured, nearly 1,700 of them steamers, 1,575 electrics and 936 powered by what were called "hydrocarbons."

Everywhere there were bicycles, cable cars, horse-drawn ice wagons, surreys and men on horseback. But a pattern was shaping. On Thanksgiving Day, 1895, a Chicago newspaper had sponsored a "motorcycle race." The winner of the fifty-two-mile junket through blizzard and snow drifts was a curious hybrid called a "buggyaut" (sic), a four-wheeled buggy with a two-cylinder gas engine steered by a tiller. While onlookers jeered and other contestants complained, it had won at an average speed of five miles per hour. It was the beginning of the auto race.

Yet such mechanical eccentricities were viewed with general alarm and fear. Typical was the editorial stance of the Los Angeles *Times,* which reported on September 1, 1901, with apparent delight, that a steam-driven "mechanical man" named Hercules had "run amuck" at Cleveland's Forest City Park. This horrendous Frankensteinian mechanical monster was described as "eight feet tall with a plug hat and fiendish grin." It "belched fire from its nostrils" when the oil was lit inside. Small wonder the unfortunate onlookers had fled in terror! The newspaper also reported a local automobile incident. "A couple of men," the paper's correspondent in San Diego reported, "had arrived in San Diego at 12:29 P.M. Tuesday, having left Los Angeles the previous Saturday at 6:30 in the morning. They selected the mountainous roads and hardest grades to test the machine," the item explained, "and traveled 200 miles. The machine stood the trip admirably . . ."

Southern California, like the rest of the country, was feeling the first touches of the new national optimism. There were still less than 350,000 people in the area, while settled northern California boasted 1,150,000. But Los Angeles seers already had that glint in their eye as they bartered acreage with one another.

The great tide of health-seekers and low-income old people which had engulfed the area between 1870 and 1900 was waning. And local boosters were doing everything to discourage them. Southern California had the questionable claim to fame as the "sanitorium belt" of America, and Eastern financial interests felt the economy was built on nothing more than the pennies of indolent invalids. Who would want to back industry, real estate and agriculture in a land where Chinese herb cures and sun-basking were the major trades? Needless to say, it was hardly an economy geared to automotive venture.

General Otis, publisher of the Los Angeles *Times,* sounded the clarion call about that time in an editorial. Among the people who shouldn't buy a railroad ticket to Los Angeles, he growled, were "dudes, loafers, paupers, those who expect to astonish the natives, those afraid to pull off their own

6

PLATE *2* *Early motorists often banded together to render mutual help on long runs.*

coats, cheap politicians, business scrubs, impecunious clerks, lawyers and doctors." The old warrior-booster then went on to explain to skeptical Easterners that "Los Angeles people do not carry arms, Indians are a curiosity, the gee string is not a common article of apparel here and Los Angeles has three good hotels, twenty-seven churches and 350 telephone subscribers."

The Los Angeles Police Department had new uniforms along with orders from the Chief to "keep your coats buttoned, stars pinned over left breast and outside of coat, and hold your clubs firmly." In 1900, too, the LAPD had organized a Bicycle Squad to police the residential areas.

Indeed, the immigrant ill were declining, thanks perhaps to the "impecunious" doctors who had come to treat them. But the final craftsman, the undertaker, was in full glory.

One British observer, Horace Bacall, noted in 1900 that "In Southern

California, funerals are like the Irish wake, a source of entertainment to the many who attend them. If the deceased happens to have been in his lifetime a member of any order, his funeral becomes a public function, a parade. You march to the burial ground clad in the uniform of your order; a band furnishes appropriate music."

Still, the unhappy sick who had been the nucleus of southern California's growth did not disappear overnight, even though communities fought a rearguard action, showing open hostility at times and spreading tales of tuberculosis epidemics. Local laws were passed discriminating against invalids and oldsters with small incomes.

Such a climate was hardly one to nurture sales of autos or appeal to a sportsman set. The *Times* ads of 1901 offered a variety of more direct appeals such as "Dr. Wong's" medical cures and a variety of quackeries including items to "cure the morphine and opium habit." One could buy a nickel bottle of "Carter's Hair Restorer" which "restores gray to natural color and replaces fallen hair." Moth balls were seven cents a pound and Lola Montez cream, a miracle concoction to revive youth, a shocking 35 cents. Canadian whiskey was $1.00 a bottle, shoes $3.95 and the better men's suits $9.55. There was a lively trade in bikes, surreys, baby carriages, two-horse milk wagons and camp wagons. But not a single auto ad!

Obscure notes of the auto, however, were finding their way into print. When President McKinley was shot by anarchist Leon Czolgosz, he was rushed to an improvised operating room at the nearby fairgrounds in Buffalo in a "motorized ambulance." The day after he died, a dispatch from the same city reported that an auto race had been called off due to the national calamity.

Los Angeles bustled about in wagons, buggies and on bicycles. Five years earlier the first interurban line from Los Angeles to Pasadena had gone into service and an electric line from the city to Santa Monica had been completed in 1896. The horsecars of the 1880s were gone. Road maps showed bicyclers where to journey and the affluent affected fancy surreys and carriages. On Washington's Birthday, 1900, twenty-nine contestants teed off at the city's first golf tournament at the new course at Western and Pico, and one observer returned from the East to report that "the growing popularity of golf throughout the country will eventually bring thousands to live in Southern California. We must be ready. . . ."

The year indeed was the turning point from a town to a metropolis. The city had 102,478 people, a startling increase of more than 100 percent in a decade, and a boom from a population of only 11,183 in 1800. Henry E. Huntington was to be the catalyst in 1902, when the onetime San Francisco railroad tycoon bought into the Los Angeles Railway Co. He was to spread this complex to tie all of the small communities together by electric railroads. Real estate values soared as people could, for the first time, comfortably explore a ninety-mile radius. By 1904, the first moving picture film ever shot in Los Angeles, showing a dirigible in flight, was exhibited; four years later, the first movie, "In the Sultan's Power," was to be released. Even as it looked to the bright future, Los Angeles discovered its past. A Union Oil Company engineer discovered the prehistoric fossils in the La Brea Tar Pits while exploring for oil. But it was to be 1907 before any effort was made to dig them out.

It was against this backdrop that our ten young men started their automobile club. A bewildering array of activities in the next twenty years, the generation of hydroelectric power, agriculture, oil, mining, manufacturing, was to bring the auto more and more into importance. The noted California historian, Robert Glass Cleland, was to note years later: "It is safe to say that nothing ever influenced California life and society so spontaneously and so profoundly as automotive transportation."

Still, the significance was born slowly. In 1907, the politicians did not yet realize the import. Governor Pardee's message to the Legislature that year made no mention of the auto when he spoke of the need for good roads. Rather, he saw their benefit in "the saving of money in horse flesh, harness wagons, time and draught power." The first paved highway in California, constructed especially for motor traffic, was not to come until 1912, and the auto, butt of jokes and humor, in most of the state was restricted to eight miles per hour in residential districts, six in business districts and four at intersections as late as 1910 when there were 36,000 vehicles in the state. Quite naturally, the men who started the Club were defiant believers banded together in mutual protection against the reactionary horse-and-buggy set then in control.

We can get some clue to the character of the group in the recollections of Henry Chamberlain in WESTWAYS (May, 1953) in which he speaks of his father, first president of the Club.

Lee Chamberlain ran a firm known as the Pacific Automobile Stables concerned with the sale and repair of automobiles. (The word "garage" hadn't yet drifted over from France.) Merchandise included electric horseless carriages, runabouts, stanhopes and a large four-seated machine known as a brake. Recalls the son: "Though they were beautiful, the darn things wouldn't run more than a matter of a few miles at a time." It was the elder Chamberlain who suggested to cronies at a luncheon that they form a club, predicting the day that there would be "at least a hundred" autos in Los Angeles.

If Chamberlain was a starry-eyed dreamer, he also paid the price. His "Stable" went broke later and he moved to the more secure field of the iron business, becoming the agent for the newly founded U. S. Steel, for Colorado Fuel and Iron Co. and the Robert Dollar Steamship Co. But we get another vignette of his persistence from a conversation that took place in his home a few years later. Mrs. Van Nuys, of the pioneer family, mentioned that some friends were thinking of moving to those distant orange groves known as "Hollywood." Mrs. Chamberlain ventured the theory that it would take a large stable of horses to get in from such a remote place. Colonel Isaac Lankershim, who must have been a wild-eyed dreamer of a sort himself, replied that horseless carriages were going to be a success and in a few years the trip from Hollywood to Los Angeles would "only take a few hours." While other guests were wiping their eyes after guffawing at that idea, the elder Chamberlain interjected. "You wait and see," he said. "They now have automobiles that run by steam and even by gasoline, and we have fifteen members in our automobile club."

And indeed the grand little group was apparently under way, although the early record-keeping was casual. No entries were in the one volume of minutes of the meetings from December 16, 1900 to April 4, 1903. The Club seems to have been in some sort of suspended animation. The probable reasons: very few autos (the first state registration figures were to appear in June, 1906, showing 6,428 vehicles); secondly, the early autos were so unreliable as to be really toys; third, streets were such that even if one had a horseless carriage, there were few places to drive.

But the Club re-organized with a flourish in 1903, electing officers, adopting by-laws and articles. (One curious early rule outlawed dealers in self-propelled vehicles from membership.) Entrance fees were set at $25 for the first fifty members and $50 thereafter, with $24 yearly dues.

On this memorable evening fifty-six members actually signed the by-laws, but two signed twice.

Growth was slow. "Official" garages for members were named. A series of automobile tours, races and runs were held and members, all of amateur standing, took part in local parades.

Some of these joyous affairs must have been exciting, indeed. Frank Flint in his St. Louis runabout won the Redlands endurance race on June 20, 1903, in three hours and twenty minutes. A run from the city to Santa Monica was held in September, details unreported. In April, 1904, the Club members conducted a run to Pomona with forty-two autos participating; members of the Board of Supervisors were honored guests and a luncheon followed at the Hotel Palomares. ("All but one auto made the round trip," the records proudly note.) In May, 1904, the Club directors were involved in preparing a grand parade, inviting the mayor, chief of police and other worthies. Divisions included gasoline and electric runabouts, electric vehicles and utility wagons and delivery trucks. Some 210 vehicles took part in the great event led by the Catalina Island Marine Band blaring out rousing march tunes. "One of the grandest and most unique spectacles ever presented in the City of Los Angeles," opined one observer. After the event, Club officers convinced the chief of police that four, eight and twelve miles per hour were prudent rather than the lower city limits. The law was changed.

The first Club race was held in November, 1903, at Exposition Park under the rules of the American Automobile Association. The official program lists fifty-six members of the Club, but fails to tell who won. But in October, 1904, a two-day event at Agricultural Park, rented for the occasion, was held on the one-mile dirt track used for Sunday sulky racing. A series of heats and finals, five miles each, was covered by local newspapers. (That same year the intrepid Barney Oldfield, with full throttle and no muffler, roared down this same track, skidding around turns while spectators cheered.)

But the 1904 event showed a growing maturity. There were strict rules to qualify and such prizes as the Huntington Cup, the L. P. Lowe Perpetual Challenge Cup and the International Open. Too, there was excitement aplenty. In the Huntington Cup Race one George Fuller of San Francisco with a Pope-Toledo was pitted as a favorite against Frank Garbutt, a Club director, in a special auto he and his mechanic had built.

PLATE *3 In 1903 and 1904 the Automobile Club sponsored races in Agricultural Park, now Exposition Park.*

Before the race, Garbutt covered the mile track in his homemade auto in fifty-eight seconds, within two seconds of the world record for a circular track. Talk of the great race the next day was everywhere on Friday, October 21. But, alas, tragedy struck! Fuller's Pope-Toledo caught fire while awaiting one of the races before the big event. Newspaper accounts explain the auto would have exploded had a mechanic not rushed out and "broken the tank open with a plank." The Huntington Cup Race was postponed until the next day. In a miracle of improvising, Fuller's auto was patched up and entered, but Garbutt won with Fuller coming in second.

A verbal donnybrook of sorts took place that same day, also. The leader of the San Francisco club protested at the judge's stand, alleging discrimination. It seems the auto of one Dr. J. D. Hill of the Bay City was barred from the race on the basis that it was being driven by the good doctor's chauffeur. Dr. Milbank Johnson, referee, held that the rules clearly stated the driver had to legally own the auto which was entered

12

as well as be an amateur. Paid chauffeurs and professional drivers were outlawed. What was more, the doctor noted at the time, the Huntington Cup was probably the most valuable racing trophy in the U.S. and not to be taken lightly. (Oilman E. L. Doheny's Peerless was disqualified for the same reason in another race that day.) That same year the Club emblem was also adopted.

Yet, while chauffeurs were seemingly being discriminated against, the Club saw the desperate need for them. In February, 1905, noting the inefficiency of such paid drivers, the Club directors proposed a school of instruction at the YMCA. In November it was started with a $1,000 appropriation by the Club's Board. It was a stunning success.

Dr. Johnson, one of the stalwarts of the Club and twice president, quit in 1905 for "personal and professional reasons" and Garbutt resigned as a director the same year. Both apparently quit in harmony and "regretfully" and continued to pop in later.

By 1906 the Club was a solid organization and the move to take it into the mainstream of southern California life was in full flower. No longer was it for a small band of sporting bloods. A meeting that year clearly indicates that both the auto and the Club had come of age. The by-laws were changed to establish an entrance fee of $5.00 and annual dues of $1.00 per month. What was more, even auto dealers were recognized as respectable and it was decided they, too, could join. (But they still couldn't be Club officers.)

Ahead was an entirely new concept: the Club would not only be of direct aid to members—but to all motorists and communities where the Club had taken roots. Ahead, also, was five years of startling growth and service.

Chapter 2

STAND BACK NELLIE

First Man: "I can't understand the rising generation.
My son wants to be a racing driver."

Second Man: "Well, I shouldn't stand in his way."

—Joke, 1906

THE YEARS between 1900 and 1917 saw the auto accelerate from a playboy's toy to a national necessity. It was as if Barney Oldfield himself was pushing the gas pedal as the speed increased. The first six years of the Automobile Club of Southern California seem to have been marked by exuberance combined with an unqualified conviction that the auto was the greatest invention since the free lunch.

Historians continue to ponder the moot question of whether men make history or history makes men. Whatever, the Club founders were apparently ready when history turned the crank of the horseless carriage. For between 1906 and 1911, the Club was to burgeon from a few hundred enthusiasts to 3,200 serious motorists.

A variety of factors were at work which would combine to sparkplug the automobile revolution.

The Pure Food and Drug Act was made law in 1906. It ended the wild quackeries and claims in public advertising and gave advertising in general increased dignity and importance. With this change came a new role for the mass circulation magazines which would serve manufacturers as vehicles for nationwide advertising in the years ahead. It was an era of trademark and symbol and automakers were quick to cash in. Other merchandising capitalized on the growing role of the auto in American life. Murine told the public that the soothing potion was "a tonic for auto eyes" brought on by dusty excursions. Saks and Co. of New York offered a luxurious waterproof auto coat of rubber and silk for the mesdames at an extravagant cost of $42.50, while even BVD got on the motoring bandwagon with warm unmentionables for the gentleman, "knee length drawers" which wouldn't creep or crawl up while he was at the wheel.

Progress was everywhere in that lusty year. One firm offered an artifice for the more daring ladies eager for an hourglass figure. In was a "pneumatic bust form" designed to lure and deceive the gentlemen. In addition to sex appeal and "doing away with unsightly padding" the tricky garment had a final function. "At the seashore," the manufacturer boasted, "the pneumatic bust acts as a buoy to the bather and makes swimming easier." For the indoor romantic the Edison Phonograph was available for $10 and up (records, 35 cents) and one could cavort to "two-steps, waltzes and quadrilles in dancing tempo." Cawston's Ostrich Farm of Pasadena was in the fashion swim selling ostrich feathers for milady's bonnet at prices ranging from $2.25 for nine-inch tips to $25 for "a two-yard boa of male plumes." One could buy rubber storm aprons with head holes to cover five occupants in an open auto and beer advertising didn't shilly-shally in its claims. "Now you can get a beer without that skunky taste," one brewer announced. Goodrich offered fine "stud tires" which were encased in "imported leather" with steel studs.

As for the autos of that era, several score were available. Such names as have passed into history were on every autoist's tongue. One could buy a Walter, Imperial, Cleveland, Bates, Kansas City, Craig Toledo, Premier ("New York to San Francisco and back to Omaha without one stop!" the ad claimed) or a vehicle unhappily named the "Klink," which sold for $1,850 including "a tri-tone horn."

The excitement of motoring was making news. In 1903 the first cross-country tour had been made in fifty-two days. In 1908 six cars set out on a westward race around the world from New York to Paris. It became an endurance contest as our heroes fought their way over game trails from Wyoming to the Coast and later across roadless Siberia. Three of the starters made it, with the winner reaching Paris in five months, eighteen days. Also, a lively debate broke out in 1909 over whether an auto was a "he" or "she." Paris—arch-citadel of fashion—favored "he." But Americans decided an auto was a "she," like a ship. (A typical ad for Reo proclaimed: "She's a Pleasure Car—for all who ride her.") While Indianapolis Motor Speedway spread garish posters in 1909 of "death-defying drivers" at "the greatest race course in the world," milady could take solace in an invention of the Ball brothers, a dashboard device for cranking the auto which eliminated the unseemly and immodest task of grinding away in front of the radiator. (By 1911 another milestone was reached with the Kettering self-starter which helped eliminate the risk of a broken arm.)

Meanwhile, back at our Club, the starry-eyed enthusiasts were still at it. Real estate man William May Garland, president during 1906–07, set businessmen to chortling over their shaving mugs by predicting a population of a million for the city someday. Similarly, oilman G. Allen Hancock, later to become a famed philanthropist, who was president for the next two years, kept things humming with his intense interest in road-charting and sign-posting. Presidents George Ellis (1909–10) and Roy P. Hillman (1910–11) added more impetus to the burgeoning activities.

Record-keeping was still hit and miss. But in February, 1909, the first issue of *Touring Topics,* later to become WESTWAYS, was published and was to serve as a lively diary of goings-on.

Touring Topics (ten cents a copy, $1 a year) was no frivolous under-taking. It announced its stern goals in the first issue: to provide activity information in detail; to promote motorist's well-being; to avoid favoritism in behalf of dealers or manufacturers. It chronicled news of highway bonds, road conditions, traffic laws, even while it touted scenic wonders and sportive tours.

Our petrol pioneers were collaring cronies at every turn in their effort to build the Club. In January, 1908, there were less than 300 members, but sixteen months later more than 1,000 motorists or fans were signed up and the annual income must have soared to $16,000 from entrance fees and dues. Still, it was pin money for the projects ahead, such as the announced Tour Book.

The first Tour Book (388 pages) in 1909 was a grand affair which included nearly 100 maps of roads in southern California and the coast to San Francisco as well as descriptions of Club road signs, their locations, and state and city traffic laws. It took time, also, to boast of Club economics ("It pays no salaries, or office rent, its entire funds are applied directly toward the work it advocates . . .") and outlined the previous two years' accomplishments, which included spending $12,000 on some 1,400 direction and danger signs for motorists and contributing $2,000 toward building Pasadena Boulevard. A. S. C. Forbes who, with his wife, was later responsible for placing the mission bell replicas along El Camino Real, also wrote an article on the King's Highway. Two years later another edition of the Tour Book supplied more maps of routes through the San Joaquin Valley to the Bay City.

Other ambitious ideas took form. The Club started recommending hotels and garages with Club insignia. But apparently some weren't up to snuff, for the practice was abandoned between May and August, 1910, and an effort was made to recover the insignia. Then recommendations were resumed with lists of the establishments carried both in *Touring Topics* and the 1911 Tour Book. Too, a chauffeurs' registration bureau

PLATE *4 The old plank road near Yuma, Arizona.*

was started and evolved into a program of free listings for drivers and potential clients. (An editorial in 1912 asked members to report any unsatisfactory drivers to the Club.)

Headquarters shifted constantly in those years. First, simply a free cubbyhole in one director's office, the Club later was moved twice on Hill Street and then settled in a new office on Olive Street. One project went astray when in October, 1910, members were allowed to use their cards as bail if arrested. But the agreement with the chief of police was gradually discontinued a year later.

Fun and games were still the major preoccupations and races and parades were frequent. The April 23, 1910, Club Run and Barbecue

20

was typical. That bright morning 227 autos gathered in front of the Club headquarters and set forth chugging merrily toward Malibu. We shall never know how many successfully forded the streams and jiggled down the narrow beach roads to Topanga-Malibu-Sequit Ranch. But enough weary adventurers gathered in the sycamore grove to listen to a twelve-piece orchestra and eat sizzling beef and beans to make it a memorable day. There were joyous footraces for both men and women and a baseball game between the "four cylinder" and "six cylinder" men, something akin to motorboat fans playing against sailing enthusiasts today. A fat man's race and a sack race added to the fun.

The Touring Information Bureau came a year later. In those green years preparing for a trip afield was comparable to checking today on skiing conditions for an upcoming weekend. Sudden washouts and various disrepairs on the dirt trails were commonplace. But the Bureau, it was declared, assured "absolutely reliable" data for the adventurous. A few months later still another service was added. The Secretary of State approved the idea of the Club issuing auto licenses. A callow stripling, Frank Jordan, was given a desk and $75 a month to handle the chore, and at the year's end he proudly announced that one month's receipts had soared to $1,357. What was more, he was apparently so intrigued with the role of the politician who approved of the Club issuing licenses that he later became California Secretary of State himself—and still is.

The auto driver, if no longer part of a persecuted minority, was still subject to scorn and hatred in the rural reaches. And police kept a wary eye on the noisy newcomer to city roads. The Club's attempts to aid motorists who became too sassy or carefree at the wheel were cautious. It was, after all, trying to win the help and respect of law enforcement officials.

One director, attorney Charles L. Batcheller, acted as a sort of adviser, digesting traffic ordinances for publication in *Touring Topics*. In 1911, members were notified that the Club's lawyer would aid them only when an auto was stolen or when they had suffered an "unjust traffic arrest."

But that same year another Club crusader emerged. He was young attorney Edward Kuster, who had been elected a director. When a Club member was arrested for speeding by our boys in blue who had hidden themselves beside the road with a stop watch, Kuster decided it was time for a showdown. He went to court, protesting "speed traps." History neglects to record whether he won that case, but Kuster officially started the Club's legal arm on November 21, 1912.

Still, it wasn't until 1923, after continuing Club complaints, that the state formally outlawed the practice of speed traps.

The judicial complexities involved in the emergence of the auto as a fact of American life were just beginning. The first state action had been a casual bill in 1905 requiring chauffeurs to have licenses and auto owners to pay $1.00 for a registration seal. The state vehicle law that year included a few basic rules of the road regulating overtaking and passing and setting a basic speed law of 10 mph in "built-up areas," 15 mph in towns and 20 mph in the countryside. But a jurisdictional conflict soon developed. Each community had its own idea about how to regulate the newfangled contraptions. Los Angeles, for example, in 1909 had speeds of 6 mph at crossings, 8 mph in tunnels, 12 mph downtown and 20 mph elsewhere. As for the unhappy motorist, he not only had to concern himself with ruts, tardy pistons and wandering livestock, but had to weave his way through this maze of conflicting speed laws and zones.

The Club constantly grumbled about this crazy-quilt system and *Touring Topics* made regular mention of the problem. Directors and police met seeking some solution, and, at the same time, the Club condemned reckless driving and road racing on public highways. The fight was to go on for fifteen years before the legal stew came to a boil. Then the Club forced the issue. A test case was taken by the Club's legal department to the state Supreme Court in 1920. The supremacy of the state laws was upheld and local ordinances in conflict were ruled invalid. Communities, however, could pass ordinances which were supplemental to state law. Hence, the Club brought about the beginning of uniform traffic laws.

By 1911 the legislature added several other bits of auto law. Motorists had to stop after an accident, drunk driving was made a misdemeanor and killing or injuring a person when driving drunk was a felony. But, in the same session, an effort to increase rural speed limits from 20 mph to 30 mph was vetoed by the governor after he heard farmer-lobbyist complaints.

The days of the carefree "I'll bet I can beat you on Sunday" race were disappearing. By 1909 permits for official races were issued under strict conditions by the American Automobile Association, which was made up of 200 clubs in thirty-two states with a total membership of 25,000.

Such a race was sponsored in 1909 by the Automobile Dealers Association of Southern California under the watchful eye of the Club and the AAA. The course for the Santa Monica Road Race, as it was dubbed, was eight miles down Ocean Boulevard to Nevada Avenue (now Wilshire Boulevard) to the Soldier's Home (now the Sawtelle Veteran's Administration complex) and back down San Vicente Boulevard to the ocean front. The winning driver that year chalked up an average speed of 64.45 mph. By 1912, when some 100,000 people gathered to watch the gallant racers on the same course, the average speed for the winner had soared to 78.5 mph.

We have record of another big annual event, the Phoenix Race, held in 1908 and several years thereafter. The winner of the 1912 race, Ralph Hamlin, tells in *Touring Topics* of his adventures in his Franklin, fording stream and fighting sand. He notes, with pardonable pride, that he was doing 65 mph when he spun through Pomona. Despite a number of breakdowns, no one in the eight autos was injured and Hamlin won in 18 hours, 22 minutes.

By 1910 the Los Angeles area was dotted with Club signs. A full-time employee had been assigned to the task of making them the year before and some $30,000 had been spent over the five years since it first became one of Hancock's pet projects. They were more than useful guides. They served as constant reminders to every traveler of the role of the Club.

But still another effort was well afoot. In 1903 Club directors had outlined the "Duties of a Consulting Engineer" in their plans, boldly stating his duties and function. The only trouble was, they didn't have a consulting engineer. It was to be a decade before the role was filled. Meanwhile, directors fought a never-ending battle for better roads. One typical letter in 1909 implored the Inspector of Public Works in Los Angeles to do something about the condition of Vermont Avenue. "This street is worse than any river bed could possibly be after a freshet has torn it to pieces," a director of the Club complained. The Inspector replied shamefacedly that it was true, but said work was under way on part of the avenue.

By then the pastoral calm of the city was rapidly vanishing. In May, 1910, the City Council passed a resolution to try to solve the puzzle of crowded downtown streets. It called for the prohibition of switching or reversing streetcars between 7:30 A.M. and 9:00 P.M. and asked for

PLATE 5   *A channel iron bridge over the Santa Margarita River on the Coast Route to San Diego. The bridge was built for the Automobile Club in 1910.*

strict regulations limiting the clutter of tamale and peanut stands on downtown streets.

The increasing number of the autos across the land had created a myriad of other problems. One was simply that few engineers knew how to build roads which would stand up under "fast" auto traffic. In 1908, the Club helped in the fight for a $3,500,000 bond issue to improve and build county roads. But finding men to do the work well was something else again. In 1911, local worthies made a grandstand play. They imported a Massachusetts engineer who had won a reputation in the science of road building and put him to work.

But the Club's campaign for good roads wasn't always a bowl of cherries. It had some paradoxes. For, while the Club desperately wanted better roads, it also wanted money to be spent for the best purpose. In 1910, the first state highway bond issue of $18 million was approved by the voters, calling for a complex of 3,052 miles of roads running generally north and south through the state in the Sacramento and San Joaquin valleys and along the coast and tying into county seats.

The Club opposed this bond issue. The state would, by the measure, take over without compensation various southern California county roads being built with county funds already allocated. Further, the same counties would have to pay interest on the state indebtedness. It was double taxation. And, to add insult to injury, there was no clear explanation of how the roads were to be built or how they were to be maintained. The Club's stand was futile. But in two later bond issues the Club's call for clarification was heeded.

By now the Club was no longer considered a collection of sporty fanatics. Its suggestions were taken and by 1911, it had a network of men in various southern California counties to work on the affairs of the moment as consuls. What was more, there were four full-time employees in the main office, as the annual report that year proudly noted. The report also told of the publication of the second Tour Book, new signposting and the $2,500 voluntary subscription from members to help build the Rincon causeway between Ventura and Santa Barbara.

In the East another court fight brought on by the new way of moving about was being settled. It would be a major factor in the growth of the Club. In 1911, an eight-year patent fight ended. George B. Selden, who had built a two-cylinder internal combustion machine back in 1877, had been suing Ford and others, claiming that all auto manufacturers should pay him a royalty. The U. S. Court of Appeals ruled otherwise. And for the first time financiers could think seriously about mass-producing the auto. They were crazy things. But they seemed to be catching the public's fancy.

Chapter 3

A NEW FORCE IN THE LAND

"Nothing has spread socialistic feeling in this country more than the automobile; to the countryman they are a picture of arrogance of wealth, with all its independence and carelessness."

—Woodrow Wilson, 1906

In 1911, the Club had 2,500 members. By January, 1920, there were 30,320. Why this explosion in growth? Population was one factor. Southern California had 900,000 people in 1910 and, by 1920, more than a million and a half.

But subtle forces were being born during these fruitful years; indeed, an unrecognized economic revolution was under way. Politicians were unaware of it and even the capitalists, the revolutionists themselves, did not seem to recognize at first what they were doing.

It went roughly like this:

Wilson, when he accused the auto of being (if you will forgive the expression) the vehicle of creeping socialism, was thinking in age-old and traditional terms. Wealth, until then, had been something *static,* made up of things which could be saved and stored. But the new wealth, found in both electricity and the internal combustion machine, was not a *thing,* but energy or motion that could not be saved. Industrial leaders, who had access to it, could profit from it only by conferring it on the average man and persuading him to use it. Capitalists could profit only by selling the tool to create this energy to others. With this realization came a still more revolutionary recognition. Adam Smith had held that by traditional theories of wealth a worker should be paid the lowest wages he could be persuaded to take. Slowly, practical capitalists saw a new horizon: workers should be paid as much as possible to become maximum consumers of the same capitalist-created goods. With this radical idea, Henry Ford was to start the five-dollar day for his workers, which created a wild furor. "Labor" was not only made up of workers, but users, he reasoned. And so began the great diffusion of this new wealth.

Few realized what was going on. William Jennings Bryan and Robert M. La Follette continued thinking of wealth in the old way, trying to restrain capitalists and to incite the man with one horse to dislike the man with two and hate the man with an automobile. The capitalists were busy at another chore. They were trying to persuade the man without any horse to buy an internal combustion machine and have the equal of twenty horses. Historian Mark Sullivan, writing of this underground revolution, noted: "Had all the proposals of restraint ever devised by Bryan and La Follette been enacted into law, the sum of their effect—assuming the effect would not have taken the form of disaster—would not have procured for the average man even a tiny fraction of the enrichment that Henry Ford conferred upon him. . . . Hardly anything so disarmed the appeal of socialism in America as the wide diffusion of the automobile, a diffusion so general as to be practically universal." Woodrow Wilson no doubt realized the folly of his words of 1906 before he died in 1923, when nearly every "countryman" had a flivver of his own.

Yet, few men of that decade understood such elaborate concepts. Reaction to the auto had changed from churlish fury or gaping delight to casual acceptance. The horse was still very much with us. A Wichita, Kansas newspaper in 1914 proudly reported the acquisition of a span of horses, "said to have cost $450," for the city ambulance. Still, the twilight was deepening. A classified ad of the time called for "Four sober, industrious men to learn auto repairing," and still another offered "a lot of good, second hand buggies, surreys, and spring wagons." But there were poignant tidbits from the other side. The Fargo *Forum* in North Dakota carried a drama of frustration in an ad announcing: "For sale: Velie 30 auto—drove from Illinois; on account of roads I cannot drive it back." Another proud, fashionable item was merchandised to rurals: "Second hand Cadillac will carry 1,330 pounds and pull like a team of horses." How true this pastoral practicality was! An auto half the weight of a horse could do sixty times the farm work without need of rest and for an unlimited time.

Angelenos were being lulled by more sophisticated sales approaches by this time. The Franklin was offered in ads of 1914 with lyrical reference to a twelfth-century Strassburg clock and its fine mechanism, while two urbane clubmen peered down at a Stoddard-Dayton from their library haven in another advertisement as one remarked, "That's the next car I buy!" The Daniels ($7,450) was portrayed next to a Russian wolfhound and chauffeur, while, for the lusty set, a classic ad showed the Jordan Playboy spinning into the western sunset with the line, "Somewhere west of Laramie." The ad went on to enchant with the explanation that out where men are men "there's a bronc-busting, steer-roping girl who knows what I'm talking about . . . the truth is the Playboy was built for her . . ."

Whatever the lure, autos were being touted everywhere. Wisconsin seemed destined to be the center of the new industry. By 1914 there were 1,258,000 autos in the U.S. and the Ford plant, where the assembly line had been introduced the year before, was striving to turn out 300,000 a year. No one is sure today how many brand names were produced. One close estimate is 2,200. The reason for the confusion is apparent. For example, one firm, The Wahl Motor Co., offered nameless cars in 1913 so that the dealer could put his own monicker on the radiator cap.

Progress continued. In 1912 the first motor truck, a Packard, crossed the U.S. It carried a three-ton load and left the East on July 8 and arrived in California August 24. This truck, it was happily announced, was being used "in 137 lines of trade in 205 cities."

Also, during those expansive years vehicles were made which were—as all such noble experiments are inevitably dubbed—"ahead of their time." The Duck was an oddity introduced in 1913. Its questionable claim to automotive fame was that the driver sat in the back seat of the open touring car while passengers sat in front in folding chairs. The 1914 Studebaker offered hickory wheels with detachable rims, while the 1914 Scripps-Booth had electrically operated pushbutton doors. Still other flamboyant items were the Octoauto of 1911 with eight wheels, and the Reeves Sextauto, with six. Another oddity came in 1912 when the American Locomotive Company tried to blend the lure of the railroad with that of the auto by producing the Alco, which had Pullman ventilators in the roof, illuminated steps and ten-inch-deep upholstery.

During this wild and exciting decade of expansion, experiment and changing economics, the Club was to find itself deeply involved in new activities and with an ever-increasing role in community affairs. Fred L. Baker, a director, took over as president during these halcyon days. And while the greatest membership growth was to come in the final three years of the decade, jumping from about 10,000 to over 30,000, many activities and decisions were under way earlier. Auto registration in the state reflects the mood. In 1912 there were 76,669 cars registered and by 1920 the figure had soared to 604,187.

A trailblazing move in 1912 was, without doubt, the gesture that would put the Club in the eye of the whirlpool of auto activity. This was the decision to start the Interinsurance Exchange. A curious dilemma had developed. Old casualty companies were still wary of the auto as a source of insurance business. There was no accurate way of appraising rates and what little history there was was so unstable and changing as to make predictions dangerous. Hence, as no one could ascertain what to charge the insured motorcar owner, rates were sky-high. By 1912 these extravagant rates were proving a gold mine for the insurance firms and the unhappy motorist, who wanted some form of protection had no recourse but to pay. The Club directors decided to investigate the economic subtleties of "interinsurance," which had been authorized by state law the year before. Stripped of involvements, it allowed an individual to get insurance from an "attorney in fact," either an individual or a corporation. The Club decided to give the venture a try and the Exchange was organized as a separate legal entity which was obligated to pay expenses and losses from premiums and not be directly associated with Club finances. (Through the years it has remained much as it started.)

As might be expected, insurance interests attacked the Exchange with an array of charges and rumors. Some predicted quick bankruptcy and word circulated that dire things were in store for anyone who subscribed. But the total effect became apparent in a few years as more and more motorists joined up. The board insurance companies had to lower their rates to compete with the idea the Club had started. Hence, motorists throughout the state were the ultimate winners. A few years later, the Club developed liability insurance handled through a private firm.

Meanwhile, the earlier preoccupation with sign-posting and road-charting kept apace. Charting of several routes from the Mississippi River to southern California was completed. A 1913 report heralds the activity. The Club had covered 3,495 miles and placed 4,510 signs on 3,474 posts on main highways and bought a road-charting truck. (By the end of the decade a fleet of such trucks was active.) By 1914 there was an entire staff busy putting up new signs and replacing those destroyed.

One of the Club's ambitious chores that year was to sign-post the National Old Trails Route from Los Angeles to Kansas City with the financial aid of other agencies. Under the Club's initial drive, every county on the route helped in the project. Some nine weeks were spent planning sign placement. It was decided, *Touring Topics* of August, 1914, notes, that some 4,000 signs would be needed. They were installed on metal posts and showed the distance to the nearest large town in each direction. The purpose was not only to lure tourists to California and to help motorists enjoy an eastern trek more, but also to promote Club prestige. A crew

PLATE 6 *Early road conditions demanded hardiness in motorists: arriving at the top of Casitas Pass was a triumph in 1906.*

PLATE 7 *Exploring San Dimas Canyon in 1917 was a "dampening" experience.*

of three initially set out in a special truck and fought blizzards and desert heat and sandstorms.

Other projects under way in those years included covering the Midland Trail from Los Angeles to Ely, Nevada, and part of the Lincoln Highway from there to Omaha, Nebraska. During 1918–19 attention was turned to the Arrowhead Trail route from Salt Lake City through Las Vegas and Barstow to Los Angeles. Most signs were white enamel with blue lettering, diamond-shaped, although some were rectangular. They included mileage and directional signs in addition to such warning signs as "Dangerous Curve," "Water—Fill Up" and "Warning. Speed Limit 15 Mi. Per Hr. Close Muffler." All were made by a Los Angeles bathtub firm. The cost of these projects over several decades totaled more than a million dollars.

Growth and activity were everywhere. The first district office was established in San Diego in 1913. "Branch offices," as district offices were then known, replaced the earlier consuls.

The Club faced a potential threat on this front during its growth period. Auto groups in such towns as Santa Barbara and Ontario were emerging, planning their own clubs. There was the danger that a variety of ineffective auto clubs would come into being unless all such organizations could be brought together. But Santa Barbara residents set the trend when twenty-two motorists joined the Club in 1911. The danger of small groups without common aims and support disappeared.

Promotional activity was keeping pace. In 1912, a public speaker went to work, visiting larger towns to seek the aid of prominent locals in increasing Club membership. As part of the drive, *Touring Topics* started a series of articles on different counties to encourage tourism. Along with the sign-posting, road-charting and the Club's reputation for fighting for better roads and highway bond issues, local communities found themselves constantly allied with the Club. The need for the district office network was established. These first offices were usually in hotel lobbies or chambers of commerce. But gradually the Club leased quarters of its own.

From 1916, when the move started with local offices in El Centro, Visalia and San Bernardino, growth was steady until there were twenty-two by 1920. *Touring Topics,* again, was to regularly report the functions of these outposts, which gave the same services and informational aid as the main office in Los Angeles. Further, the district offices watched local road progress in each county and filtered in such data as daily road reports, cross-fertilizing their activities with headquarters.

In those distant days when "public relations" was still an unknown phrase in the land, the Club recognized the need for the public to know what was going on. Los Angeles *Times* publisher Harry Chandler, a Club director, was asked to seek out a newspaperman to build a publicity department. Allied to *Touring Topics,* the new office sent out a steady flood of releases dealing with southern California motoring and Club activities, which often made daily news.

Inevitably, as the auto emerged as a standard part of the American scene, the plunderers came. Stealing an auto had been a rare event when they were few. Any thief knew his prize would stand out like the proverbial sore thumb on the local landscape, and "exporting" a stolen auto was a task for a hero, not a thief, in those times. Now organized bands emerged, stealing accessories and the vehicles themselves. The Theft Bureau was organized by the Club to aid the police, working with the legal arm in prosecutions as well as with the Interinsurance Exchange in the fight to keep lower insurance rates.

The Club's annual report for 1918 stated that since the Theft Bureau started operation in 1915, it had recovered 979 cars for members of the Club and the motoring public. "The Theft Bureau . . . is kept open twenty-four hours a day the year around, and a motorcycle officer, ready for instant service, is on duty all night at Club headquarters."

In 1918, the Club reported: "Two uniformed officers of the Club are on duty each night during the theater hours keeping watch over automobiles parked along the streets adjacent to the show houses. In addition, these patrolmen notify the car owners of parking infractions and attach cards to steering wheels notifying motorists of flat tires, et cetera. Many letters commending the Club have been received and it seems likely that it will become so popular that a greater number of patrolmen in the uniform of the Automobile Club will be employed."

Allied, also, to this new service were the lost and found department started in 1915, a forwarding department in 1916 to arrange rail shipment of autos for members and, in 1918, the all-important emergency road service. The first tow truck was originally assigned to the task of only bringing in wrecked or stolen autos of members, but not those with mechanical troubles. Later that same year, a twenty-four-hour service for members whose cars were disabled on the roads was started without charge. Infuriated towing operators complained. The Club briskly replied that it would "decide what service to render members." In 1919, still another flourish was added with a special Club car stationed at Yosemite during the touring season to obtain road condition information and render emergency service.

There is no question that this colorful decade was to firmly establish the Club as one of the major influences on California life. The days of the daring youth adventurers had passed. During the next decade, the Club was to fight hard for better roads.

Chapter 4

THE TUMULTUOUS TENS

"Mr. Motorist: It is up to you to give persons on foot a courteous, friendly warning—a danger signal which will not rob them of their presence of mind. Many a tragic auto accident is due to the inefficient 'Honk-Honk' or the terrifying squawk signal that alarms and unnerves pedestrians and makes them RUN INTO DANGER—instead of AWAY FROM IT."

—Ad for the musical horn, Aermore, "the Horn Harmonious," 1913.

IF THE decade to come was to be known as the Roaring Twenties, the decade before it was the Tumultuous Tens in the history of the automobile. Manufacturers, buyers and pedestrians were indeed scampering in all directions as the advertisement for "the Horn Harmonious" suggests. Frantic growth and confusions dominated.

By 1913, a furious fashion fight involving the auto was under way. The question at hand: Do milady's automobile styles really originate in New York or Paris? *Automobile* magazine took an editorial stand on the matter in its issue of January 14, 1914: "Even the most patriotic American will admit that motor styles originate in Paris. The small-town Middle Western merchant looks to Chicago for his idea in style. Chicago goes to New York, New York depends on London and London gets its ideas from Paris."

The same magazine, a sort of Emily Post of motoring of the time, had put down its dictates on auto etiquette a short time before. The real season for the chic to start automobiling was September, it ruled, and the correct wear included rubberized auto coats, dust-protecting veils and English tweeds.

Strange spectres were loose on the land which would change the manners and technique of the autoist. Mack Sennett was at work in Hollywood by 1912 with his immortal Keystone Kops, who were to immortalize auto driving with comic verve. In 1913 a small monster was quietly born in Washington, D.C.—the personal income tax which affected so few Americans that humorist George Fitch dismissed it with a shrug, noting "it will be an exclusive circle, this income tax class— one which the ordinary . . . man cannot hope to enter."

War in Europe brought a boom in farm prices, which created an urgent demand for autos and farm equipment to meet the market needs. At the same time Billy Sunday was expounding his muscular Christianity and Tarzan began to cavort in print and angry arguments waxed over the corset as a health menace. It was the heyday of the player piano and the tango was turning the country topsy-turvy. At Indianapolis the speed records continued to soar: Joe Dawson, driving a *National,* won the 500-miler at an average speed of 78.72 mph. The *Lozier* Metropolitan was "the choice of the men who know." It was a glass-enclosed $4,450 sedan with a single door in the middle of the body as well as an electric starter and lights. The "three p's," however, were the ultimate in motordom—the Packard, Peerless and Pierce-Arrow.

The electric starter was having its own kickback. Cadillac started experimenting with it first in 1911. By 1919, self-starters were optional on most autos. The days of the "starter arm"—a fracture of the right forearm caused by the unexpected kick from cranking—were past. The spark plug, subject of endless debate among avid motorists, was in its full glory. There were some twenty-seven major brands on the market with every motor owner claiming he had bought the best. Too, the snobbish lure of things Continental, which had always made insecure Americans feel nervous, was being promoted in motoring circles. Common talk went, as always, that Europe was producing the best autos and the Keeton was typically advertised at $2,750 as an auto which was "a European type—at an American price." Still, the U.S. was holding its own in offering something for everyone. The 1912 Kissel was a "semi-touring" car, for example, that was "roomy for four but not over-crowded for six."

Angelenos were busy with the joys and pangs of growth. In November, 1913, some 10,000 proud locals gathered to watch the first water pour forth from the $24,500,000 Los Angeles Aqueduct while the famed soprano Ellen Beach Yaw sang, "California, Hail the Waters." They were talking about the revolutions and counter revolutions across the border and about the U.S. citizens being killed on this side by stray bullets. Angelenos launched a major city cleanup campaign as tourists streamed into California for the San Diego and San Francisco expositions. Los Angeles streets were decorated with huge tubs of palms and trellises of blossoming roses. That memorable spring the city's schoolchildren also put on the "March of Empire" pageant when the Liberty Bell, enroute from San Francisco back to Philadelphia, was placed on exhibit in Los Angeles.

The Club was deeply involved in all such goings on, unofficially debating such thorny questions as whether the San Fernando Valley might possibly develop into more than an agricultural area with the new supply of water and what roads might be needed.

Wars and rumors of wars had little impact on southern California at first. But, as the decade wore on, the effects were felt in the needs in Europe, particularly in agriculture, where farmers realized the role of the auto in increasing production and harvesting.

As the Club grew in community life, it was inevitable that conflict, debate and quarrel with other ambitious entities would come.

One of the livelier disputes came when the Club and the American Automobile Association failed to see eye to eye on who was to run what.

The first trouble started in 1912 when motor dealers and others promoted many races under the banner of the Western Automobile Association. This group was organized under the leadership of Frank Garbutt to hold races independent of the AAA Contest Board. The AAA wrote the Club asking for aid in preventing this disregard for the AAA Contest Board in southern California. In April, 1913, an arrangement was made to organize a group to be known as the Club's Contest Committee, and also to be the AAA representatives in the area. Five would come from the Club and five from the maverick WAA group. This new local contests committee would use the AAA national board rules as well as control all auto racing in the area.

Conflict between the AAA and the new local group was almost immediate. The AAA insisted every item of business be referred to the national board. The local committee found such an arrangement impossible. Time lags and the fact that expenses were being carried by the Club, with all racing fees going to the AAA board, created bitterness. The Club sent the AAA a detailed letter of complaint. The AAA in New York made a few concessions but, during 1914, Club directors became more unhappy over what they considered the domineering policies of the AAA and its Contest Board.

When the AAA asked the Club to give up all its maps of the National Old Trails route for the AAA to publish, the Club refused. In March, 1915, the chairman of the AAA Contest Board arrived in Los Angeles and announced abolishment of the local contest board and plans to appoint one full-time AAA contest representative. People in other parts of the country felt the local contest board had too much power and had complained to the AAA, he claimed.

The fat was in the fire. In a lengthy resolution on March 18, 1915, Club directors formally broke all alliances with the AAA. Two years later the AAA was to try to tie the knot again. But the Club refused. The efforts at reaffiliation were to continue for thirty years. But the old bitterness remained.

Despite such high-level disaffection, fun continued at a lively pace. A schedule of two runs a year to attract members was voted by the Club in 1912. One colorful three-day event that year was the run to San Diego and return with a barbecue and athletic events. Another was the 170-car run to Santa Barbara to celebrate the formal opening of the Rincon Causeway. The trip was one day up, and one day back, with the autos widely separated, rather than in parade formation, due to the dusty roads.

In 1915, there were three runs to San Diego to visit the San Diego Exposition. In one of these events three groups set out, one on the coast route and two on the inland route, with two trucks following each cadre,

PLATE *8   Between 1911 and 1914 the Auto Club was headquartered at Eighth and Olive.*

which also boasted a motorcycle escort. In April, 1915, the same run was made with 247 autos, the largest array yet put together. The Thanksgiving Run that year to celebrate the opening of the San Diego–Los Angeles highway was grander still, with 500 vehicles involved.

But the advance in such highway glory was short-lived. We find that the planned run for February, a few months later had to be called off due to the road and washed-out bridges. Even by then the idea of a run was declining as a motoring concept. Safety in numbers was no longer so great a need. Individual motorists were more and more willing to venture forth alone.

The storm of war hit the U.S. in 1917 and the Club was soon involved in a variety of efforts. In addition to Liberty Bond sales, collecting supplies for the Red Cross to send to Belgium, encouraging food conservation and remitting the dues of Club members in the service, it called upon members to help out in the myriad activities of war on the home front. Members acted as chauffeurs for workers in campaign drives, carried speakers from place to place and even hauled aliens and slackers to the courts for the authorities. Not without significance was the fact that Army recruiters were sent to Los Angeles early in the war to recruit ambulance drivers. It was a questionable tribute. For it seemed that southern California auto drivers were more adept and better trained in dodging the ruts and shell holes they would find in Flanders than the city slickers of the East Coast.

Naturally, the war's needs affected all Club activity. Auto production was turned to military need and skilled mechanics were in great demand for war work. Auto racing was prohibited by the federal government and gas sales were restricted. Too, highway construction was all but stopped during the war and for some time after, due to an embargo on railroad equipment. The flatcars were being loaded with war materials rather than the items and equipment needed for road work. March 6, 1919, found the Club anxious about this. A resolution was sent to the Legislature asking that $3 million be diverted from the general fund for highway construction and to give work to returning doughboys. Again, a few weeks later the Club asked for a constitutional amendment to provide for a third state highway bond measure to expedite this work.

The Club faced new problems in every field. In 1912, it had already become apparent that new means had to be devised to meet mapping services. Issuing tour books every two years was unsatisfactory: too many new roads and even new towns dated them almost immediately. The solution was a system of separate area and strip maps to keep pace. Maps were issued of scenic routes, of routes to national parks, of beach towns and of coast and inland routes north. But the demand was never-ending. The annual report for 1915 shows that the Touring Bureau answered 50,000 calls in the main office and 25,000 in the district offices. During one heavy storm there were 1,200 calls in one day. In 1918, Touring Bureau inquiries averaged 440 a day and a million maps had been printed that year.

Yet, even with the auto a transportation reality, conservative elements fought a rearguard action. In 1912, the Club brought an action challenging the state's 20-mph speed limit. Motorists felt the main purpose of the law was to get revenue from traffic fines. The year before, Governor Hiram Johnson had vetoed a measure approved by the Legislature allowing 30 mph. Motorists felt this unfair. The test suit was lost, but in 1913 the maximum speed was raised to 30 mph. That same year an elaborate new vehicle code was enacted which included registration fees based upon a vehicle's horsepower. This, the Club felt, gave the state too much arbitrary choice and favored a flat $3.00 annual fee. A test action was filed. But the Supreme Court ruled against the Club and it was 1923 before the law was changed to a flat fee of $3.00.

In 1915, the state passed a law with vague provisions about headlights. The Club had faced another issue in 1912 when Los Angeles tried to compel motorists to buy a certain patented device for speedometers which showed in colored lights what speed one was driving. This set a firm Club policy: opposition to any laws requiring motorists to buy particular patented devices.

A vast array of other proposals for Club activity came before the directors during those years. They included a number of requests for Club cooperation in road building projects; aid in preserving wildlife; support for various auto shows and fairs; a study to regulate jitney buses. The Club was in favor of these.

But the Club declined to become involved in routing of a state highway or to endorse commercial emergency service for motorists. It backed away from endorsing political candidates, the purchase of an oil

PLATE *9 In 1914 the Club began the ambitious job of sign-posting the National Old Trails Route to Kansas City.*

well and a request that mercantile discounts be obtained for members. And these were but a few of like propositions offered.

Road building, as mentioned, was a massive activity during these years and the Club was deeply involved. As an example of growth, *Touring Topics* noted that in 1900 there were 231 miles of paved street in the whole city, but by 1913 there were 726 miles, while in the county that year some 300 miles had been completed from the bond issue of 1908. Between 1908 and 1920 every county in southern California voted road bond issues with the Club active in the fight in nearly every instance. By 1919, more than $19 million in county bonds for roads in the area had been voted.

State highway financing was under constant pressure. In 1910, there were only 3,052 miles of state highway, mainly running north and south. The bonds for these were most difficult to sell on the open market because interest payments were only 4 percent. The counties stepped in to buy enough of them so that the balance could be sold. A series of bond issues to come, totaling $73 million, led to 5,607 miles of highway by 1919.

Yosemite Valley was closed in 1907 to autos and in 1911 the Club led a fight to reopen it. In 1913 it won the fight—with the payment of fees and tolls and the understanding that not all Valley roads would be available to autos. But Club activity did not end there. By 1919 the Club had raised almost $20,000 to construct an all-year road in the Valley. It was finally completed in 1926. In 1914 the Club endorsed the use of convict labor for road work and a year later it promoted a scenic drive from the head of the Arroyo Seco to Cajon Pass. In 1919 Club directors held more meetings in support of the Arroyo Seco and Angeles Crest Highway—though the latter project was not completed until 1956. The Club was active in federal planning, too. Since 1912 it had been sending a representative to meetings in Washington on highway affairs. Growth was everywhere.

By 1919 California motorists had 5,806 miles of paved road on which to frolic.

As the decade of the teens drew to a close, the auto was a fixture of American life. The first Model-Ts, which had come out in 1908, were still humming merrily about. But many motorists knew little about the autos they were driving. Home mechanics were disappearing.

Between 1915 and 1916 the number of autos manufactured had almost doubled, from 825,930 to 1,525,578, even as Henry Ford turned to tractor production to gird for war. The first enclosed Model-T came off the assembly line in 1917, as did the first mass-produced auto wrecker with crane. By that year there were 4,700,000 autos on U.S. streets, an increase of 58,650 percent in just seventeen years, for in 1900 there had been only 8,000 cars. What was more, the tide had only started. For, after all, wasn't Henry Ford producing a fine car for as little as $345, FOB, Detroit?

Ahead for the Club were still more golden days—and one of its major battles in the public interest.

Chapter 5

THE GREAT HIGHWAY FIGHT

"Gentlemen, you face a tough job! You are expected to build for $18 million a highway system that the best engineers of the country have estimated will cost from $35 million to $50 million . . ."

—Gov. Hiram Johnson's comment to
new state highway officials in 1910.

W<small>HEN</small> Johnny came marching home in 1919 he found bleak days. For two years depression haunted the land: some five million unemployed; 130,000 Gold Star emblems hanging in the windows of the mourning; shelves stocked with goods no one could buy and factories which had over-expanded during the war years now muted and silent.

True, there were some 4,000 U.S. millionaires more than before the war, a total of 20,000. But there was labor strife, the postwar dollar was worth less than half of the prewar dollar, housing was scarce and everyman's dream—an auto—was an expensive luxury.

Controversy and debate racked the country. That most annoying segment of humankind—the women—had become even more emancipated during the war and now demanded all sorts of special rights. The great army of tipplers groaned in abject despair when the 18th Amendment took effect at 12:01 A.M., January 16, 1920.

During those years argument flurried over whether it was cruel to keep Socialist leader Eugene Debs in jail, and fisticuff fans grumbled because Jack Dempsey was still pondering his next fight twelve months after his win over Jess Willard. Boston banned "The Birth of a Nation" and, about the same time that the first coast-to-coast phone conversation was held, Babe Ruth was picked up for speeding, fined $100 and spent a night in the sneezer, but was freed by an understanding judge in time to play the sixth inning the next day at the Polo Grounds.

But grand things happened to the postwar autos. The trend was toward snob appeal. Such touches in advertising as the luxurious Biddle display simply showed the auto and the name, apparently feeling further comment was unnecessary. The Owen Magnetic claimed it would "banish the commonplace" and was recommended as "necessary to a successful social season," showing formally attired passengers with chauffeur.

Jack Dempsey, the hero of controversy, posed in his luxurious disc-wheel McFarlan, one of the largest and most expensive autos, to anger fans even more. The 1920 Premier boasted something new: shifting was done electrically by a lever on the steering wheel. But luxury aside, every young man's dream was a glistening yellow Kissel Kar with sloping windshield and rakish body. No girl could resist a kiss in such a sporting transport, legend held.

To be exclusive and distinct was the automakers' battle cry. Don Lee in California cashed in with custom-built body designs offering such unique custom items as a touring car on a Rolls-Royce chassis. One prized Lee creation was a slope-hooded roadster on a Renault chassis for Fatty Arbuckle and another was a two-door sedan with mahogany interior on a Cadillac chassis. In 1920 the first try to sell jewel-precision, little autos at high prices, came with that "superfine small car," the Templar. A sedan cost $3,785. It didn't catch on.

Despite the economic slump the auto industry produced 1,905,560 autos that year and Henry Ford, temporarily $50 million in debt due to expansion, caught the tide with the famed "Tin Lizzy," which was to become the top seller. Gadgets and metal trim came into their own with nickel-plated lamps and radiators, and the 1922 Paige had the first white sidewall tires.

The grandest of all was the Stutz Bearcat. Bright red, yellow or blue, it had a three-speed transmission mounted on the rear axle and cost $3,500. It boasted a trunk for two suitcases, two extra rear-mounted tires and wheels, parking lights, windshield wings and upholstery in "the finest hand-buffed Spanish leather." The man who owned a Stutz Bearcat had achieved nearly everything and there was little to look forward to in life—except next year's model!

Southern California was bustling and the economic woes of the East weren't felt with the same impact. People uprooted by the war or looking for the second chance began to appear in increasing numbers with savings and occupations. The Club itself was booming almost from the end of the war.

The Club was fortunate during those trying postwar years, too, in that it had a remarkable array of executive talent to guide it through the shoals of adjustment. The president was Fred L. Baker who, in February, 1920, was reelected by the directors to serve for his tenth year. Also president of the Baker Iron Works and later president of the Los Angeles Steamship Co., he was a man of zest and drive. His energy was limitless. Prior to his tenure as Auto Club president, Baker had served as president of the Los Angeles Merchant and Manufacturers Association and two terms on the City Council. He had been a member of the Water Board

PLATE *10 In the post-World War I years, the popularity of the automobile burgeoned. Henry Ford's "Tin Lizzy" became the top seller.*

during the hectic period between 1905 and 1908 when the great Owens Valley Aqueduct project was aborning. He was also chairman of the board of Los Angeles Shipbuilding and Dry Dock Co. and Los Angeles Lumber Products Co. during his busy career. Yet, despite his schedule, he was in almost daily contact with other directors pushing the Club forward. A robust and handsome man, he left the presidency in 1921, but continued on as a director. In 1926, he was elected the sole life member of the Club.

Others at the helm during those trying years were of equal ability. Allan C. Balch, who served as a director from 1911 until 1939, was an engineer and a founder of the Pacific Light and Power Co. A man of remarkable organizational talents, he headed many standing committees during his twenty-eight years as a director. Another was Joseph F. Sartori, who first became a director in 1922. He had organized the Security Bank in 1890, which was to become years later the giant Security First National Bank. He directed the legislative committee of the California Bankers Association and was one of the founders of the Los Angeles Country Club as well. For over four decades he remained a major leader in the development of southern California.

Still another long-term director was Harry Chandler, publisher of the Los Angeles *Times,* who served from 1913 until his death in 1944. This forceful southern Californian was active in scores of enterprises. He was a trustee of Stanford University and California Institute of Technology, a director of Associated Press, as well as a director of some forty different California corporations involved in agriculture, banking, manufacturing and other industries.

During those years the Club directors, who have always served without pay, had a routine pattern, met once a month for dinner at the Club to discuss policies and activities and plan ways to meet the problems of growth, and were in constant consultation between the meetings to settle matters.

And growth it was! On December 31, 1919, membership stood at 30,320. By the end of 1924 the rolls had swelled to 104,355 active members.

With such burgeoning activity came, of course, the need for more staff members. Records are skimpy, but we can get some clue to this employment statistic from annual reports. In 1914 there had been about fifty employees. By January, 1919, the total stood at 130 and in March, 1922, the payroll had swelled to 500. Many of these early workers in the Club vineyard were to stay on into the 1960s.

No one could accurately chart in those early postwar years exactly what the destiny of motoring might be. It was, of course, much more than a sport by now. It was tied into the entire national economy. But predicting how many auto owners would pop up in southern California in the next decade was a nigh impossible task.

Some indication of this can be found in the dilemma of creating a Club headquarters during those hectic years. In 1914, the Club leased a 50-foot lot at 1344 South Figueroa Street and built a two-story brick building with basement and a garage in the rear. Four years later the directors acquired an adjacent lot and put up another building, almost a duplicate of the first. Yet, two years later, it was obvious the expanding needs of the Club had already exceeded the real estate required. In March of that year property on the southwest corner of Adams and Figueroa streets was acquired. Additional parcels were added to this original purchase in 1921 and 1922.

Debate swirled about where to go from there. It was even suggested that an eight-story building be constructed. But this wild idea was voted down. A three-story concrete headquarters with basement and garage was built and occupied by 1923. By 1930, another expansion was necessary. An addition of about the same size was added to the original building. It now serves as headquarters, the nerve center of Club activity today.

All this was achieved by a series of loans and mortgages paid off gradually over the years. It was of particular pride to the directors that it was done without tapping membership dues, but by brokerage income received from the placing of members' liability insurance.

Expansion was everywhere during those early years of the wild 1920s. Bill Henry, the present Los Angeles *Times'* columnist ("Window on Washington"), became editor of *Touring Topics* in 1920. He nurtured the publication to an ever-increasing size until 1926, when the late Phil Townsend Hanna took over as editor.

New departments emerged. The commercial car department was started to aid operators of commercial vehicles. It struggled with the intricate problems of business and industrial motorcars for two years. But disagreement arose over the ever-present controversy of load weights. The Club held that 22,000 pounds should be the maximum weight limit for four-wheel trucks to properly preserve and protect the highways. Commercial operators felt otherwise. The law allowed 30,000 pounds as a maximum and they weren't anxious to lower their payloads.

A public safety department was added and an abstract bureau proposed in 1921. J. Allen Davis, an attorney with the Los Angeles County Counsel's office, took over the latter to start issuing certificates of title on the purchase of new and used vehicles. But, after several months' study, it was decided the Club shouldn't become involved. Davis moved his activities to highway and motor vehicle problems and became an associate counsel.

By 1922, the requests for information about camping, hunting and

PLATE *11* *The Club was busy mapping and sign-posting for the new motorists.*

fishing also led to the establishment of a bureau, which later became known as the Outing Bureau.

Meanwhile, the woes of urban motoring were growing apace with the joys and convenience. In 1922, a study was started by the Club's consulting engineer, J. B. Lippincott, into ways to relieve traffic congestion in Los Angeles. The report which was issued only verified the obvious about the booming city. Mushrooming growth and subdivisions created out of individual ideas rather than long-range coordinated planning had led to dead-end streets, to quaint and curious jogs in roads and to general chaos. As some sort of solution for the quandary, Lippincott suggested one-way traffic on Fifth and Sixth streets, the removal of obstructions at intersections, street widening and cutting through a number of dead-end streets. At the same time the conflict between the steam engine and the gas engine revealed itself in the problem of grade crossings. A long-range program unfolded to eliminate rail and highway crossings wherever possible.

It was but one of an array of Los Angeles' problems which came with an ever-increasing traffic flow and population explosion. In 1923–24 the Club cooperated with the Los Angeles Traffic Commission, a civic organization, in preparing a comprehensive survey of the city's traffic problems. Results showed Los Angeles had a much smaller percentage of downtown area devoted to roads than other major cities; the report called for the widening and opening of a number of side streets to serve as new traffic arteries and recommended legal methods and legislative measures. (The city kept trying to implement the relief measures up through the building of the freeway system. But the problem continues. The opening and widening of surface streets to take pressure off today's freeways during peak traffic hours goes on.)

Yet the greatest issue faced during the opening years of that decade was the state highway crisis.

The massive problem came about as the inevitable result of previous legislation that had failed to provide the funds needed to build roads described in bond issues. Many miles of good county roads had been constructed, but the state highways were too few and of poor quality. To add to the snarl, the historic and powerful northern part of the state had obtained a disproportionate amount of state roads compared with the south, even though the major population increase was here.

Politicians, business leaders and engineers all tried to attack the thorny problems of how to get all the roads and highways that were needed with the funds allowed.

They tried, but the dollar would stretch only so far. The question was whether to build more miles of low-grade highway or stick to high standards and fewer miles of road with the funds available. The Governor and Highway Commission chose the former—low-grade construction, but more miles of it, trying to get the auto out of the mud. It was short-term improvising. Some state highways started falling apart only months after completion.

To add to the problem, the state failed to enforce truck weight laws and, with added use of trucking, the destruction of roadbeds grew drastically.

The Club fought strenuously during those fateful years, urging engineering reports and postponement of the building of added highways and roads until the existing main arteries were brought up to recognized standards. But pork-barrel politics were at odds with limited, high-quality construction and repair. Both the Governor and Highway Commission ignored the Club's pleas. A report issued by the Club and the California State Automobile Association in 1921 highlighted the dilemma. It noted that political scandal or waste or extravagance was not at fault. Yet, it went on, four-inch pavements were breaking down in four and one-quarter years, long before the bonds that had been issued for the same highways had been paid off. Lack of preparation of sub-soil and drainage facilities, insufficient foundations, and thin concrete—all added up to the weak policy of trying to get as many miles of highway as possible for the dollar invested.

The State Highway Commission continued to defend its policy, calling for a gasoline tax in 1921 for additional finances. But tests made by the two Clubs only confirmed the conclusion that California was proceeding to build more bad roads. Their battle with state authorities stretched into 1922. Relief finally came in 1923 when a new governor was elected and a new highway commission appointed.

With the change came new legislative measures for highway construction and the first gas tax of two cents per gallon, with one cent going to counties and the other to the state for highways after administrative expenses were paid. While counties could spend the funds for maintenance or construction of roads, the state had to restrict spending to maintenance, repair, widening and reconstruction of state highways and roads in state parks. In effect, all the gas tax funds were used to catch up with and repair the damage already done.

This first gas tax was a historic breakthrough and a revolutionary one in terms of highway financing. The state's taxpayer was freed of highway bonds and county taxpayers generally found the same easing of their burden. New weight fees supplemented the revenue from gas taxes and changed the whole concept of financing road building. Today, the existing highways and roads of the state would have cost billions in bond issues. Instead, the pay-as-you-go system brought a new tax era to meet the ever-increasing needs of auto transportation.

In 1922, Club attorneys prepared the original draft of a new California

Vehicle Act. By 1923, it was introduced in the state Senate as a companion measure to the gas tax bill. It provided for repeal of the horsepower tax on autos, along with the approval of the gas tax, and set a flat registration fee of three dollars for each vehicle, with additional fees-for-weight for commercial vehicles. It also reduced permissible weights to 22,000 pounds for four-wheel trucks and 34,000 for trucks with three axles and six wheels.

It had been a stormy period, these postwar years. And the Club had whizzed by a lot of important milestones. But, during those same memorable days, there was fun to be had, too.

Chapter 6

CHARTING THE ROAD TO CHANGE

PROTECT YOUR CAR AGAINST THEFT!
*Locks may be picked or jimmied. Cars may be stolen in spite of them.
BUT no thief ever attempted to steal a car with a man at the wheel!*
BOSCO'S COLLAPSIBLE RUBBER DRIVER *is so lifelike and terrifying that
nobody a foot away can tell it isn't a real live man. When not in use this
marvelous device is simply deflated and put under the seat. Easily inflated
with your hand or automatic pump. Price $15.*

—Ad for rubber dummy
to scare auto thieves, 1920.

LIFE was still no bowl of cherries for the motorist of 1920, despite such imaginative aids as the device advertised on the preceding page.

Picture yourself going to the office one winter day in that year. You may own a Briscoe or Lexington or Commonwealth. But probably you have, like so many others, a Model-T. It stands much higher than today's auto and the chances are nine to one you are warmly clothed because your car is open. (Only 10.3 percent of autos manufactured in 1919 were closed, the sedan vogue had just started.)

If you have a Model-T, you climb in the right side, as there is no lefthand door. You set the spark and throttle levers like the hands of a clock at ten minutes to three. If you are affluent or a gadgeteer you may have a self-starter, but chances are you have to get back out and crank. You slip your left forefinger through a wire loop near the radiator and pull it while you cautiously give the crank a twirl with the right hand. When the motor finally catches, you leap to the shuddering running board and move the spark and throttle to twenty-five minutes to two. If the engine is too cold and dies, you repeat the rite until it starts again. Once at the wheel, you release the hand brake, put your foot on the low speed pedal and with a surge sweep onto the street; quickly you release the left foot to let the car into high gear and you are off in a blaze of speed.

There are only some seven million passenger cars registered in the U.S. and traffic is thin. In California you can drive at 50 mph on some roads. Many are now paved. You have little trouble parking; the ubiquitous parking lots and meters of the future are unknown.

Thus it was in that romantic decade after World War I. Air-cooled engines were still around. The best was in the 1923 Franklin which, dealers in southern California claimed, had "driven through the trackless and uncharted sands of the Imperial Valley at 122 degrees for many hours without trouble."

Popular music glorified the motorcar and some twenty-nine shows dealing with the auto were brought to the stage. Hit songs included "In My Merry Oldsmobile" and later "Henry's Made a Lady out of Lizzie," which bemoaned the agonies of the Model-T and proclaimed the exciting

Model-A which offered "no more bruises, no more aches, now she's got those four-wheel brakes."

Chrysler was to become a fixture in 1924 with the "70" and offer such advances as high-compression engines, four-wheel hydraulic brakes and rubber engine mountings. Steamers such as Coates, Doble and Stanley were wheezing about in 1923.

Notables were in the automotive news. Sidney Smith, creator of "The Gumps," favored a $16,000 sports phaeton trimmed in bronze and brass with mahogany running boards. But some of the more conservative were less flamboyant. Philip K. Wrigley of chewing gum fame, who knew where a nickel came from, endorsed in an ad the 1925 Ford saying it had "the sweetest clutch I ever handled." And the price was right! In 1926, Fords ran from $290 for the runabout to $565 for the four-door sedan.

Still, luxuries were popular. Rolls-Royce overestimated this feeling and made a classic blunder in its classic manner in 1921 by trying to invade the U.S. market with a plant at Springfield, Massachusetts. It was a short-lived failure and the effort was soon abandoned.

On a smaller scale of luxury, portable radios were offered in 1923 for autos. They were in clumsy wooden cases and featured chiefly static.

During those years an array of other items concerned Americans. Sinclair Lewis' *Babbitt* created a furor and Princeton University advised parents that students need not have autos to attend school. Mr. Coolidge moved in and Emil Coué became a fad with "day by day in every way I am getting better and better." Henry Ford refused to run against Silent Cal for president and U. S. Steel abolished the twelve-hour day in 1923 and came down to ten.

Talk was everywhere of Red Grange, Loeb and Leopold, Florida real estate, Lenin's death, the sale at auction for $6,500 of Abe Lincoln's garments worn when he was assassinated. News came that an American auto had crossed the Sinai Desert between the Gulf of Suez and the Gulf of Aqaba in four hours—it had taken the early Israelites forty years to cover the same 130 miles in their Exodus from Egypt. Ford made his ten millionth car in 1924 and paid income tax on $2,467,946.

In addition to its involvement with highway legislation, internal growth and membership during those years, the Club found itself facing a more subtle influence. In the first years of the auto only the adventurous set forth against the hazards of dusty roads, broken axles, broken fan belts or the

PLATE *12 By 1925 middle-class America had leisure and the money to enjoy it. So touring ballooned.*

host of other threats. But with improved highways, the more comfortable sedan and better engines, perils diminished in the public's mind. A clue to the burgeoning interest in touring can be found in the annual report of 1923. That year the Touring Bureau answered 792,026 personal calls and 454,984 telephone calls. Also, there were 69,295 letters of inquiry and the Bureau issued over seven million maps.

All this led to the eternal questions every explorer has had to ask. What was out there? What dangers would one encounter? How long did it take?

Even at that late date U.S. road maps were haphazard affairs, pasted together and improvised with a hope and a prayer. How far was it from Two Forks Junction to Clarksville? Well, probably just short of fifteen miles the local sheriff would surmise. How steep was the grade up Dead Warrior Hill? Most cars boil over twice, the service station attendant at the foot of the hill would explain.

And so began one of the Club's most ambitious undertakings: to chart and explore the nation's network of highways and roads and bring back exact figures to make accurate maps.

In May, 1920, the first great venture was announced—to completely chart the Lincoln and National Old Trails highway from Los Angeles to Washington, D.C., and New York City. Two men of the Club staff, "Dusty" Rhodes and Ollie Lewis set out in a roadster with survey speed-ometer, compass, grade meter and altimeter. Mission: to get accurate de-tails on every mile of road. "The biggest task ever undertaken by a single motoring organization," opined *Touring Topics* with pardonable pride.

The daily log shows that between May 17 and July 14 our adventurers covered 8,881 miles of road, chronicling road signs, altitudes, conditions, grades and distances. When the data strip maps were drawn, there was available the first truly accurate guide for Club motorists anxious to take the great leap and Drive East.

Another expedition set out that same year. Donald Doig, manager of the Touring Bureau and Elmer Brown, Club map maker, set off in a Hup-mobile touring car with the task of charting southern routes. It took four and a half months and they covered 15,831 miles. A clue to the stress and strain involved in fighting sand, swamp and wilderness can be found in repair work. The two exploreres broke seven front springs and five rear springs going through the seventeen states. They returned December 23, 1920, with all specifics on such colorful routes as the Ozark Trail, Oklahoma's Pigeon Route and Hockaday Trail. From their research came still another accurate series of strip maps.

But the most exciting mission was to come in 1921. *Touring Topics* in the June issue outlined "the greatest road-charting tour in history." The aptly named "Dusty" Rhodes and Ollie Lewis were again the protagonists in the drama against weather and rut-holes which was to last nearly five months and cover almost 25,000 miles to collect data on the north-eastern, central and northwestern states, with several exploratory stabs into Canada.

Noted the Club magazine:

"Never before has any automobile organization found itself large enough or powerful enough to be able to send two experts on a trip of such monumental importance to automobile owners . . . Mr. Motorist will be able to follow his route to its destination by means of 'strip' maps which will give accurate directions over every square yard of the itinerary. . . . A trip of this magnitude is made possible because of the support given the organization by interested auto owners in Southern California. . . . But it

PLATE *13 Car camps and camping sites, like these near San Diego and Laguna Beach, sprouted as the auto expanded the universe.*

would not be possible if the Club had not already brought its system of "strip" road maps down to such a fine point that they can be turned out with such accuracy that they are internationally adaptable."

The result of the venture was road information which, it was admitted, was without equal and available nowhere else in the United States.

Even while such ambitious projects were under way, routine mapping chores went on regularly. One of the Club's charting cars covered practically all of California, including national parks. Another appraised the state's beaches while a third went over Westgard Pass into Ely, Salt Lake City and back through Zion, Bryce and the North Rim of the Grand Canyon.

The maps, meanwhile, found new uses. In summer, 1922, a Club member, L. D. Sale, president of the Western Wholesale Drug Co., wrote of his adventures using a Club map to pilot a plane from Los Angeles to San Francisco.

Building, expanding, road-mapping and facing the complicated legislative crisis of highway construction and vehicle licensing highlighted those five years between 1920 and 1925. But there were hosts of other problems and considerations within the Club operation.

The Club worried about "hurryitis" which was infecting the Los Angeles motorist. In 1920, a Peerless set a record with a run between Los Angeles and San Francisco on the inland route in nine hours and twenty minutes. Oilman E. L. Doheny offered the Club the services of his architects who had designed the nearby Catholic church and the new Episcopal church to prepare a façade for the proposed new Club building that would harmonize with the church building. The Club did not use their services, however.

There was concern that the City Council planned to repeal an ordinance setting standards for gasoline and Club directors asked the Motor Car Dealers Association to help fight the idea. The Club organized a Traffic Vigilante Committee which started operating April 1, 1920, with 200 volunteers. They were asked to report infractions to police on forms which were signed not by name, but an assigned number. The police then warned the violators. Within a few months there were 400 volunteers reporting the most common offenses of passing standing streetcars, cutting corners and just plain reckless driving. The practice was open to abuses, however, and was discontinued.

Litterbugs were a menace in the nearby countryside and the Club started a campaign to "keep the mountain canyons clear of delinquent and deceased bean cans, pickle cartons and sandwich kimonos."

The woes of downtown traffic continued to mount and Club Engineer J. B. Lippincott reported some 22,000 cars a day were entering and leaving the city during 1920. That same year Los Angeles unveiled "the world's largest garage," a nine-story wonder at the corner of Grand Avenue and Fifth Street.

The Club was involved, too, in a plan to restore California's missions, and worked with a committee that included Herbert Hoover, Luther Burbank and Harry Chandler. But such pleasant and romantic chores were in the minority. Intricate, workaday problems absorbed daily effort. These included such concerns as the manufacturer's responsibility for auto defects, interinsurance rates, fights to preserve the yuccas, safety campaigns, theft insurance coverage, the loss-ratio statistics of collision and federal highway bills.

By 1923, a study showed that Los Angeles held the questionable record of having the most fouled-up and congested downtown streets of any city in the world. Endless Club meetings were held to devise ways, through street-widening and other means, to unsnarl the tangle. Meanwhile, sign-posting went on at a lively pace and the annual report in 1924 shows 6,622 temporary signs and 10,155 permanent signs were set up. That same year a memorable milestone was reached with announcement of the establishment of the Club's Highway Patrol Service. Patrol cars manned by mechanics trained in first aid and a fleet of light trucks were to make regular runs in Club territory to aid all motorists, the first such patrol in the U.S. The drivers' functions included hammering down spikes at railroad crossings, nailing up temporary route signs, sweeping broken glass from highways and towing in disabled cars.

By then the highways of California were becoming more and more clogged with the onetime oddity. State registration on July 1, 1924, was at 1,014,578. Some 800 different makes were on the road, but 95 percent

PLATE *14 The attentive members of the Club's original Highway Patrol searched for drivers in distress.*

of them were of the thirty-two most popular trade names topped by Ford, Chevrolet, Buick, Dodge, Studebaker and Overland. There was a total of 6,500 miles of state highway by then, but only 2,400 miles were paved.

As for Club members themselves, they had emerged as a venturesome, hearty breed out for new thrills in the expanding universe created by the auto. Titles of *Touring Topics* articles showed the flavor: "In the Valley of Graven Images" (Chiricahua National Monument), "Fighting Snow in the Passes of the Rockies," and "Ensenada the Exotic."

Along with such buzzing activity, of course, came the unhappy statistics. In 1924 a report from Washington, D.C., showed the soaring traffic accident figures for the previous year: deaths, 22,600; persons injured, 678,000; property loss, $600 million.

Yet it was all part of the great panorama of one of the greatest transitions in American history.

As the Club reached the end of a quarter century, undreamed changes had transpired in America and the world since those ten young men gathered on the chill night of December 13, 1900, to "protect the lawful rights and privileges" of motorcar owners.

Internationally, the U.S. was now a great power. But, more important, the average American's daily life had changed more radically in those twenty-five years than for any human in all history, thanks primarily to science and practical industry. Medicinal science had surged ahead. (The average American died at forty-nine in 1900 and, by 1925, it was age fifty-three. In 1900 the telephone was a luxury, by 1925 the human voice on radio could be heard halfway around the world. The motion picture, the telescope, an ever-increasing efficiency of engines converting coal, gas, petroleum and waterfalls to power added new benefits.

In 1900 the farmer survived with a few horses and his own muscles. By 1925, nearly every farmer had an auto of at least 20 horsepower and most had tractors. In 1900 the ten-hour day, six-day week was commonplace. By 1925 the middle-class American had leisure and money to enjoy it. Autos had numbered 8,000 in the U.S. in 1900. A quarter century later there were 17 million. The ten miles of concrete road in 1900 in the U.S. had increased to 20,000.

The Americans of 1925, however, took such progress in stride. It was a prosperous, booming, carefree era and the days of depression that had marked the postwar years had been forgotten.

A new sort of freedom had come with the closed car. By 1924 some 43 percent of the autos were sedans or coupes. They offered escape from parents and neighbors in any weather. You could drive to dances twenty-five miles from home. You could drink bootleg gin in one and even park in Lovers' Lanes. The auto had changed the manners and morals of an entire people.

The motorist was rapidly reaching his finest hour. He could venture forth without fear of being stuck in a mudhole. He could stay warm. He could stay clean. And, most important of all, he no longer had to be an amateur mechanic to own an auto. Indeed, by 1925 there were those who didn't even know a spark plug when they saw one!

Chapter 7

NORTH AGAINST SOUTH

"To George F. Babbitt, as to most propserous citizens of Zenith, his motor-car was poetry and tragedy, love and heroism. The office was his pirate ship but the car his perilous excursion ashore . . ."

BABBITT by Sinclair Lewis, 1922

BY 1925 a man was known by the auto he drove, and the auto manufacturer was the matinee idol of business and finance. Garages and
filling stations dotted the happy American landscape, and the auto itself
was no longer a utilitarian instrument of transport but a hero larger
than life. The invention of pyroxylin finishes for autos brought something
for the ladies—such colors as "Florentine cream" and "Versailles violet."
Balloon tires went on the market, and the auto manufacturer turned to
designers for sleek innovations and body change to capture his share of
the competitive market.

Such goings-on forced even Henry Ford to recognize that an auto
was something more than a mechanical workhorse. The Model-T continued to lose sales leadership to the rakish Chevrolet in the low-priced
field. Ford finally announced plans for a new model to replace the
beloved Tin Lizzie.

Rumors and gossip were rampant as the date for the great unveiling
of the Model-A was set for December 2, 1927. News stories reported
whispers of dealers who claimed to have seen a photo of the new Ford.
As "A-Day" approached, Ford bought a five-day series of ads in 2,000
U.S. newspapers at a record ad campaign cost of $1,300,000.

The excitement and havoc of opening day has never been equaled
in automotive history. A million people visited the Ford headquarters
in New York that day, the New York *Herald Tribune* reported. In
Detroit, 100,000 stormed the showrooms, and in Cleveland, mounted
police had to be called out. Within a week there were thousands of
orders for robin's egg blue roadsters and Arabian sand phaetons. The
unveiling of the Model-A compared with Lindbergh's flight and the
execution of Sacco and Vanzetti as a major event of the twenties.

Still, the common man's dream, the Model-A, was only part of the
vast panorama of motordom during the flamboyant and colorful years
between 1925 and 1930. Economy cars were one thing. A luxury such
as the Pierce-Arrow was something else, starting at $2,895 for the four-
passenger touring car and offering the luxurious five-passenger sedan coach
at $3,895. The Auburn, too, was luring buyers with its dual purpose
about that time. The business coupe, it was advertised, was *handy* to

buzz about town but also *hardy* for the cross-country tour. Lieutenant Leigh Wade, the round-the-world flier, was setting another record as a promotion for Packard. He drove a Packard Eight 3,965 miles from Los Angeles to New York without once allowing the motor to stop. Now forgotten are the Locomobile, the Vauxhall, the Diana, the Gardner, Ruxton and Roosevelt. The luxurious Brewster, a forgotten jewel of body work, glittered briefly and then was taken over by Rolls-Royce.

The Club, at this time, had become very active in automotive affairs in southern California. With the massive changes wrought by the auto, the politician was recognizing the reality of the auto as a major force in the land. In 1924, Governor Friend W. Richardson had appointed a nine-man Highway Advisory Committee, including the Club's chief engineer, to get some reading of what was ahead for the state's motorists. For a year they traveled the entire highway system by auto, attending dozens of local meetings to hear suggestions and complaints. By 1925

PLATE *15 Despite southern California's shortchanging in funds, road building continued apace. Here is Fallen Leaf Avenue in 1928, now a section of Foothill Boulevard in Monrovia.*

they submitted their majority and minority reports with findings and recommendations.

In essence, the study highlighted the clear fact that southern California was getting the short end of the stick. Out of 6,500 miles of state highway, 4,124 were in northern California. The total cost was about $140 million with some 43 percent of the highways still unimproved due to inadequate funds. It would also take $217 million more to bring all designated state highways up to snuff, concluded the state highway engineer.

Both reports went on to point up the glaring inequities between north and south. About 63 percent of the highways were in the north and expenditures of state and federal funds had been 66 percent in the north and 34 percent in the south. Further, this policy of unequal development had been in effect for the previous twelve years. Improved mileage totaled 2,307 miles in the north and 1,135 miles in the south, and there was no definite, fair policy of legislation to control how the state highway commission allocated funds. Simply stated, northern California legislators had more power in Sacramento than their southern brethren and were taking full advantage of it.

What was more, the study showed, if the $217 million to bring the highways up to standard was ever obtained, plans called for about $144 million of it to be spent in the north and only some $72 million in the south.

It wasn't exactly a firing on Fort Sumter, but echoes of the report were heard throughout the state. Suggestions for a remedy varied. To raise the needed revenue it was thought by some that vehicle owners should face increased taxes for license plates by a graduated weight tax, or that the gas tax should be increased, or there should be a combination of both. The majority report concluded this would bring in an added $10 million for the year 1926 with proportionate increases as more autos hit the highways. Further, the report called for classifying state highways under a primary and secondary system with the primary system getting not less than 75 percent of funds. It also called for ten connecting roads, totaling some 190 miles to be added to the system, but came out against a plan for 3,000 miles of state highway, mainly in the north.

The minority report, submitted by the Club's chief engineer, Ernest E. East, was quite different. It suggested the state highway system be divided into a District One, made of forty-five northern counties, and a

District Two, the thirteen southern counties, with approximately 52 percent of the state's area in the north and 48 percent in the south. East went on to suggest that the state highways be designated either primary trunk lines or district roads, with the trunk routes approximately equal in north and south. The state trunk lines, he concluded, should be financed by the state as a whole by bonds for purposes of construction and by motor vehicle taxes for maintenance and reconstruction. But the district roads should be financed by the district in which they were, he asserted. The reason? According to traffic need, the south was equal to the north, and some fair and just system had to be worked out for all sections of the state. This, East said, was the best remedy.

The board of directors of the Club heartily approved East's minority report.

But the previous month a different move had taken place in the state legislature. A measure was introduced calling for an increase in the state gas tax from two to three cents per gallon, with the additional revenue from the increase to go to new state highways. It was a northern California ploy and the idea was to use the gas money and registration fees under the old plan for more northern highways, including the proposed Bay Shore Highway.

A dinner was called by Club directors for February 19 at Club headquarters. The main item on the menu was some cold turkey conversation. Club President W. L. Valentine, first Vice President Henry W. Keller and David R. Faries, the Club's consulting counsel, told the gathering of legislators and community leaders of the Club's position. The inequity had to end, and southern California had to get its fair share of highways for its tax dollar. The southern area of thirteen counties comprised nearly half the area of the state, as well as now having half the taxable wealth and population. But it was paying 57 percent of highway tax revenues and getting back only 36 percent in highway expenditures.

Said Mr. Valentine that memorable evening: "Is it to be wondered that southern California is far from enthusiastic over any increase in the tax to be paid by motorists? So vigorous is the sentiment of many citizens of this section of the state against any increase, particularly under present conditions of inequity, that it may be confidently predicted that the referendum will be invoked against any additional taxation."

He protested vigorously, too, against the northern hope to add 3,000 miles of highway at a cost of $117 million when the state was faced with the problem of completing the already existing state system at the cost of $217 million.

A few weeks later the Club was prepared for formal action. It was ready to introduce a bill in the state legislature which would appropriate $5 million each year out of the state's general fund for highway construction on designated routes. Further, it proposed a constitutional amendment for districts and trunk highways and district highways, as East had suggested, and another amendment to provide a $50 million bond issue for construction and improvement of the state's trunk highways.

Governor Richardson was politically between the devil, in this case northern California, and the deep blue sea, the Southland. In April he asked the Club for a written opinion on the pending legislative bill to increase the gas tax. Club directors announced the Club would referend the gas tax measure if it passed.

Tensions ran high that month. Nearly all of southern California's legislators from the thirteen counties fought the gas tax increase. But it was apparent northern power would win. On April 22, the senate bill was passed, increasing the gas tax one cent. It was to be used for highway construction, but without any allocation to north or south or any reference to trunk routes or local highways.

The last-ditch hope to get the governor to veto the bill still remained. The Club's legislative counsel, J. Allen Davis, presented a legal analysis of the bill with its amendments to the Club president, W. L. Valentine, who wrote the governor outlining the bill's defects. The governor referred the matter to the attorney general, U. S. Webb, who confirmed the Club's analysis of the defects. He also pointed out that the new bill would repeal the existing two-cent tax on July 24 and there would be no tax income until September 30, 1925, tax the three-cent levy started. He added that some of the senate amendments on the bill, in his opinion, were unconstitutional.

The new bill was vetoed by the governor. But the complicated fight was not resolved. Yet, thanks to the legal bungling of state officials favoring the bill, the bitter fight of 1925 was won by the Club.

Northern California was not ready to accept defeat. There was a lull, during which spokesmen for the north, represented by the California State Automobile Association, parleyed with Club representatives. But by

PLATE *16 Laying pavement, 1920's style, on the Pacific Coast Highway north of
Santa Barbara.*

year's end it was apparent there would be no resolution. Compromise
seemed impossible. On February 4, 1926, the battle was joined again
when Club directors were notified that the northern club had broken off
negotiations and nothern club spokesmen had called for a series of
statewide conferences, including propaganda invasions into the Southland.

The northern club was preparing a new political scheme, launched
early in 1926. It circulated petitions for signatures and qualified the gas
tax measure for the November ballot, known as Measure No. 4, again
calling for a one-cent increase, but avoiding allocation for specific highways
or any apportionment between north and south.

The Club then countered with its own opposition measure, No. 8, and
obtained enough signatures to qualify for the ballot. It called for an
annual appropriation of $5 million from the state's general fund for
twelve years. This, with federal aid, would mean a total of $90 million
during the period to complete the present state highway system—but

without bond issue or tax increase. The measure also allocated 75 percent of the $90 million to a system of primary roads and 25 percent to secondary highways, calling for uniform development throughout the state. It created nearly equal highway districts and budgeted funds on the basis of primary mileage, while basing the construction of secondary highways on relative land area.

The northern faction's call under No. 4 was for a one-cent increase over a number of years, but did not budget any part of the income for the completion of the present system. Too, it provided no limitations in terms of additions to the highway system.

In the months that followed, vigorous campaigns were fought by both clubs. But, on the November ballot, both measures were defeated. Everything was back where it had started.

It seemed a time for compromise and arbitration. State Senator Arthur H. Breed, Sr., started a series of meetings with the Club and the northern California State Automobile Association. After conferences and study, it was finally agreed that two companion measures would be introduced by the senator in the legislature in early 1927.

The first of the measures increased the gas tax from two cents to three as the northern interests had wished. The net revenue coming from the additional cent, however, was to go into the state highway construction fund and be spent by the highway commission for the acquisition of rights-of-way for state highways and roads. The construction improvement of them would be in accordance with the companion measure that was introduced by Senator Breed at the same time. This second measure was, basically, what southern California had been fighting for in the long struggle. It allocated funds for highways, rather than money for maintenance and administration, to a system of primary and secondary highways within northern and southern county groups.

Further, the use of the funds for construction and reconstruction were spelled out. Seventy-five percent of the money was to be expended on primary highways in the north and south according to highway mileage, which was 54.7 percent in the north and 45.3 percent in the south. The other 25 percent was allocated to secondary highways, with the north getting 50 percent and the south 50 percent.

Peace of a sort came with the Breed Highway Measures of 1927. The state administration, both clubs and many other civic organizations all joined hands. The measures were passed unanimously by the legislature. The two measures also became the shifting bedrock foundation upon which many added provisions were built in highway construction in the years which followed. The three-cent gas tax and the division of funds between north and south were to remain for twenty years until the Collier-Burns Act of 1947. This Act was passed to insure increased revenue for maintenance and construction of local streets, county roads and state highways. With the burgeoning population and thousands upon thousands more autos on the highways of the state, the Act was really an adjustment to the changing times. Yet, as we shall see later, it, too, provoked a furious and bitter fight.

The Breed measures of 1927 really made no attempt to end the geographical inequity of state highways. The northern counties continued to get a higher proportion of highways than the south. But, at the time, after the long wrangle and the failure of the measures by both clubs in the voting the year before, it was the only apparent solution. Yet, unhappily, the Breed measures were to remain the focal point of argument and controversy for years to come, more for matters that they did not deal with than those they did.

The first of these flare-ups came on October 4, 1928, when Club directors were advised that the allocation provisions of the Breed measures were not being fulfilled. The highway commission was being unfair to southern California, announced Henry Keller, chairman of the Club's roads and highway committee.

Further, the state director of public works, Bert Meek, suggested all convict labor be performed on state highways in northern California for the next biennium. Then, he explained, he would appropriate out of the anticipated federal aid of $5 million, a total of $3,625,000 for the north, leaving only $1,375,000 for southern California.

Again, the Club had to gird its loins for battle. The directors ordered a vigorous protest be sent to Mr. Meek and asked the Club's chief engineer, Mr. East, to check in detail and report how matters stood. His later report of discrepancies and recommendations showed that 77.1 percent (1,771 miles) of secondary roads in the north comprised 52 percent of the area of the state, while southern California had 525 miles, or 22.9 percent of the secondary roads, even though the Southland contributed 57 percent of the state's gas tax revenue.

Efforts to remedy the situation were useless The state officials were dedicated to a status quo policy on the highway system during the 1929 legislative session.

The Club now moved to the legislature for a remedy. Senator Nelson T. Edwards and Assemblyman Chester M. Kline introduced two bills in senate and assembly proposing fifteen new roads, totaling 615 miles, for southern California.

The effort, the Club knew, involved a tactical error. The state administration and most of the state senators were on record against more roads. Even with the inequity, to give the south 615 miles and the north none was political suicide.

PLATE *17* *The Ridge Route in 1924—a major achievement in southern California highway construction. Highway apportionment was already a hot legislative issue.*

Governor C. C. Young supported a resolution calling for an orderly addition of new roads to the highway system after engineering and economic studies. The resolution also called for the additions to the secondary system to be made within the following two years, totaling between 10 and 12 percent of the existing state highway mileage. The added mileage was to be at a ratio of not less than three or four miles to the south to one mile in the north.

The Club's Edwards-Kline bills were defeated. But the resolution was to serve as the basis for appropriate legislation in the 1931 legislative session.

Hence, by 1929 highway apportionment had become a constant issue in legislative halls. Despite differences, however, the Club and the California State Automobile Association sometimes joined hands to fight common enemies. During 1929, for example, they managed with the aid of the state insurance commissioner to secure enactment of the Motor Club Act, which defined and regulated auto clubs. This was necessary because opportunists had founded "gyp" clubs in California, promising benefits they couldn't deliver in service contracts. The Act stipulated that motor clubs post securities or bonds of $100,000.

That year other legal problems were resolved in Sacramento. The California Highway Patrol was formally placed under the Department of Motor Vehicles, and officers who had served under contracts between counties and state began to be paid directly by the state and attained civil service status. Laws were also enacted requiring proof of financial responsibility by motorists who failed to pay certain traffic accident judgments. Government agencies were made liable for damages of employees operating publicly owned vehicles. Owners of vehicles were held liable for the negligence of others driving with the owners' permission, and amendments were passed calling for a two-year renewal of operators' licenses. A new type of operator's card requiring notation of serious traffic convictions was also ordered, but, as courts were haphazard about enforcing this law, it was to be repealed in 1935.

Everywhere the auto was dominating American life. In 1919 there had been 6,771,000 passenger cars in the U.S. By 1929 there were over 23 million, the most obvious indicator of Coolidge prosperity.

Automobiles had changed the nation. Towns that had prospered "on the railroad" faded and withered as the trucking industry grew. Branch lines were closed as railroads saw profits disappear with the interurban bus. The single traffic cop at the main intersection of town gave way to flashing red and green signals, blinkers, one-way streets and scores of direction signs. Highway businesses mushroomed—hot dog stands, chicken-in-a-basket, filling stations. The age of steam was gone. The gasoline age was here.

But during those same years from 1925 to 1929, while law-making problems were such a major concern of the Club, a vast array of other activities were keeping pace. And ahead loomed the horrors of the Great Depression.

Chapter 8

THE BUBBLE OF PROSPERITY

"The business of America is business . . ."

—Calvin Coolidge

IT WAS a golden era, those bouncy, carefree years between 1925 and 1929, and the man without an auto was suspected of being a miser or a ne'er-do-well. Statistics show why. Between 1922 and 1927, American wages increased 2 percent annually. The number of people who paid taxes on incomes of over a million dollars shot up from 75 to 283 between 1924 and 1926. The stock market soared while the cost of good, mass-produced autos declined. "Coolidge Prosperity" was everywhere.

The sale and manufacture of autos was a prime mover of the U.S. economy. Some four million men directly or indirectly made their livelihood in the auto boom. Already the doctrine of obsolescence was taking hold. The American with real zing and zip didn't wait until his car wore out before he bought a new one.

Other fields kept pace. Every third home had a radio, and chain stores moved vast inventories of electrical devices, rayon products and a never-ending stream of gadgets to ease household life. The Ford Gospel (high wages, low prices, standardized manufacture) was rapidly becoming commonplace for all U.S. industries, and the dollars rolled in all directions.

Two new refinements in merchandising spurred on the great buying spree. First was installment buying. The old maxims of thrift and prudence went out the window, and the American who wanted to keep up with the Joneses "established credit" and went into debt for luxuries he didn't really need. Why not? The future was rosy and life was an overflowing bowl of cherries.

Aiding the time payment trade was the hard-sell advertising man. He relentlessly pounded at the hopes, dreams, weaknesses and fears of U.S. consumers in his never-ending drive to make the sales graph soar. On the advertising pages of the nation's newspapers and magazines new folk heroes emerged, such as Addison Sims from Seattle and the chap they all laughed at when he sat down to play the piano. Onetime burly golf champs wasted away into sniveling wretches due to tooth decay, and asthmatic nincompoops were promoted and became the most popular men in town because they bought shiny, new Packards. Fads blossomed and faded: mah jong; crossword puzzles; Coué, psychiatry.

The Club, quite naturally, was deep in the midst of these exciting times. Membership continued to soar each month. On its twenty-fifth anniversary, President W. L. Valentine took time to pause in the optimistic turmoil to look back briefly. The Club had 112,000 members, he noted—more than the total population of Los Angeles when the ten young men had started the venture a quarter century before.

He also took the occasion to announce that after five terms as president he wished to retire. But he was to stay on as a director for some years.

New leaders emerged in the next five years. Henry Keller, a director since 1909, succeeded Valentine for a year to be replaced in 1927 by Horace G. Miller for two years and then attorney Edward Lyman, who served from 1929 to 1930.

There were other changes. Former president Fred Baker retired as a director due to ill health, and former U. S. Senator Frank P. Flint, a director, died at sea in 1929. In 1926, Bill Henry, editor of *Touring Topics,* moved on to the Los Angeles *Times* to be replaced by Phil Townsend Hanna, who was to become a noted California historian before his death in 1957. David Faries resigned as general counsel to be replaced by Ivan Kelso, who was to serve until 1939. J. Allen Davis, who started attending legislative sessions first with Faries in 1923, became legislative representative when Faries retired and was to fill the role until 1939 when he became general counsel—a post he held for the next twenty years before retiring.

It had been a lively twenty-five years, but the pace was brisker still, starting in 1925. The auto was, by now, not only a means of transportation but a prime factor in the economy and well-being of a people. The demand for a uniform vehicle code for the entire country had long been brewing in discussions and letter-to-the-editor columns. The American Bar Association called a meeting on the subject on April 16, 1925. J. Allen Davis went to present the Club's concepts, which he'd written the year before. Secretary of Commerce Herbert Hoover, who'd organized the National Conference on Street and Highway Safety in 1924, was clearly impressed with Davis' ideas. For on April 20 he asked Davis to serve on the newly formed committee on Uniform Traffic Laws and Ordinances. He became the legislative draftsman in preparing the Uniform Code.

The Club was involved in complex interplay with other forces in southern California by now. One was the drive to encourage tourism.

It joined hands with the All-Year Club to attract easterners with such aids as maps and information, while an endless stream of news stories and advertising went out to national publications spelling out the glories of the Southland.

In 1924, the Club's Highway Patrol Service was announced. A fleet of light trucks cruised the state's highways to render assistance. The uniformed drivers, all qualified in both automobile repair and medical first aid, served members and non-members alike. Soon the idea of Emergency Road Service became a reality, rendered on call from official garages. Both services still flourish today.

The patrol provided yeoman service when tragedy came on June 30, 1925, with the Santa Barbara earthquake. Within three hours after the quake, eight Club patrol cars with crews arrived on the scene. For a week they aided quake victims. The Los Angeles *Times* reported in an editorial that 1,084 Club employees contributed to the Santa Barbara Relief Fund. The Club suffered its own losses. Records show the Insurance Exchange paid claims of $4,445 due to the quake.

Other growth kept pace. A new Club emblem was approved which could be attached to the front of the radiator core rather than to the radiator cap, which was becoming obsolete. The emblem was given free to Club members. In the first eight months of 1925 the Club answered 74,738 out-of-state inquiries and issued 3,736,900 maps. By the end of that year, there were thirty district offices of the Auto Club. The Club president, in his New Year's greeting at the beginning of 1926, noted also that more than four million autos had been manufactured in the past year and California could certainly expect a large percentage of them.

Safety had by now become a major preoccupation due to millions of autos on the road and unprecedented traffic death figures. The Club that year authorized $5,000 for a safety film for school children and continued to pay rewards for information leading to the arrest and conviction of hit-and-run drivers when an accident resulted in death or injury.

The national concern in cutting down the death toll led at times to crackpot schemes. Typical was a legislative effort known as the "patent bumper bill." It was to be introduced several times before the special interest groups involved finally gave up. It called for mandatory installations on all autos in California of the curious bumper which had a device that would drop a metal disc containing the vehicle owner's name and address if the bumper struck anything. As the promoters saw it, this would put a quick end to hit-and-run drivers because they'd be leaving their calling cards behind. It was later pointed out that pranksters could wander the streets and "spring" a hundred bumpers a night.

That session had other colorful legislative ideas aimed at the auto world. One was a patented registration certificate which was to be sealed by the Department of Motor Vehicles. Trouble was, it would be mutilated if anyone tried to remove it when they had to.

The parade of problems which called for a Club position went on and on. A bitter fight broke out over whether prisons or private firms should produce state license plates. The Club declined to be drawn into this controversy. It endorsed, however, the stand of the Save-The-Redwoods-League, calling for the creation of a state park commission which could use both private and public funds to acquire and maintain state parks, campsites and historic monuments.

The Club went on record against law enforcement officials who jailed motorists and held them incommunicado because they had inadequate cash to pay fines. A touchy municipal problem was the controversy over the much-discussed "highway to the sea" from downtown Los Angeles. Wilshire Boulevard, which had initially been suggested, was considered wrong by some leaders. The Club set out at its own expense to find a likely alternate route which would hopefully please everyone.

The annual report for 1925 showed some 200,000 out-of-state autos had arrived in southern California. The Club Touring Bureau serviced about 5,000 inquiries a month, most of them from out of the state. Club crews had also completed road charting in Arizona.

The problem of the "boulevard to the sea" went on. One Club survey suggested the route be from Adams and Crenshaw to the Palos Verdes Estates. But, by now, the Wilshire Boulevard project was considered the most promising, and Club directors voted to back it.

A parade of ideas and aspirations by other city planners were considered by the Club. The Los Angeles *Examiner* was taken with the idea of a system of bridle paths from Pasadena to the sea. The Club was asked to initiate the project. Directors demurred, but said the Club would assist as it could. The horse was not within the jurisdiction of the Club, directors felt.

But other projects were. The effort to build public campgrounds was a never-ending concern. By 1926, the Club had appropriated over $10,-000 for various Forest Service projects.

The thorny problems of highway construction (Chapter 7) was the major issue, of course, during those hectic years. Northern interests fought valiantly for the Bay Shore Highway (the Peninsula highway from San Francisco to San Jose was the main route then), and the Club fought just as ardently against state funds being used for it as long as the main trunk system of the state was incomplete.

The scramble to promote the Southland was continual. During 1926 Club directors agreed to appropriate funds, not to exceed $12,000, for ads in the *Saturday Evening Post* to laud the area's vacation glories. About the same time the Club saw fruition of a drive started in 1913.

PLATE *18 1927: a new paved road races the old plank one out of El Centro.*

There was a two-day celebration marking the opening of the Yosemite All-Year Road, which Club engineers had first surveyed thirteen years before.

Too, the age of aviation was upon us, and the Club intended to keep pace. A Club road scout flew with Major C. C. Mosley from Los Angeles to Salt Lake City preparing a detailed map for the pilot's use— the first time an auto club had charted aerial routes, although fliers had been using the road maps for some years as an invaluable aid in the cockpit. Perhaps a less exciting but no less noble service at the same time was formation of a crew assigned by the Club to sweep glass off Los Angeles streets.

The fracture between the American Automobile Association and the Club was still unmended. The president of the AAA wrote the Club commenting that he was touring the western AAA clubs with other officials and, if invited, would like to visit Los Angeles. Directors invited the AAA visitors to a dinner which was held quietly and without fanfare. About the same time, however, there was plenty of fanfare with the announcement of the Club's new radio show, an hour every other week.

By now the Southland was booming, much to the distress of the northern Californians. At the Port of Los Angeles, annual business reached nearly a billion dollars. But the "sunny California" of the promotional pamphlets wasn't all true. One day the Club had 352 emergency road calls—thanks to "heavy fog." Still, everything continued bustling. The Touring Bureau reported a total of 1,392,704 calls and gave away nearly nine million maps during 1926. The Club's Highway Patrol covered 647,774 miles and aided 21,600 motorists.

Meanwhile, the whizzing autos were everywhere—and a lot of the new-rich owners hadn't quite learned how to use them. During the first six months of 1927, a Club's Emergency Road Service report shows, there were 20,000 calls for help from stranded motorists. Many of the unfortunates, it was noted, were either out of gas or had burned out the bearings after failing to put oil in the engine.

Growth in roads had been fantastic by any measurement. In 1912, there had been a few hundred miles of paved roads in California. Just fifteen years later there were more than 7,000 miles, while surfaced roads accounted for 18,000 more. Some 88,000 autos in the state in 1912 had swollen to 1,785,000.

Traffic deaths remained the great modern hazard. As a result of a rigorous national program, deaths among children were decreasing in 1928. But more and more adults were being killed—many from jaywalking and violation of the fifteen-mph speed zones. The Club found itself in the reverse role of the merry men who had started the organization those 28 years before, pleading with people to slow down instead of asking for more lenient speed laws. One special patrol car called "The Owl" patroled between Mojave and Bishop each night in summer to aid stranded mortorists. The "Broken Glass Patrol" recorded picking up glass from 630 locations in Los Angeles for the month of June, 1928. And some 198 garages were now under contract to the Club to aid motorists whose machines had failed.

That year the initial drive to eliminate solid rubber tires (to be made law in 1931) was under way with the Club's support, as well as an amendment to allow autos to pass on the right or left on wide city roads.

The Club realized it had to join hands with many other groups in the complicated battle for better laws and service. Western motor clubs, all members of the American Automobile Association, asked the Club to join in a conference. It was a delicate problem; the Club and AAA were still at odds. But Club Secretary S. L. Mitchell attended in San Francisco with several staff members and, with the formation of the Western Motor Club Conference, the Club became a participating member. (Today clubs from the eleven western states still meet to reciprocate in touring information, emergency road service and other aids.)

Refinements multiplied. The Club by 1929 was selling a $1.50 black enamel license plate frame with Club emblem, and among the signs atop the Club building was one to guide aviators. It pointed directions to airfields with a north-south indicator. The whole problem of aviation was a serious concern by now. Should the Club move into this glamorous field? A legal opinion said that the Club's articles of incorporation were not broad enough to authorize spending funds for an aviation department. That was the course the Club took.

The annual report for 1928 outlined progress. There were no new district offices created, but offices designed for Club use were taken over in Hollywood, Beverly Hills, Santa Monica, San Bernardino and Fullerton. The Touring Bureau covered nearly 52,000 miles, and the Signposting

Department, 226,661 miles, adding some 22,000 temporary signs and nearly 17,000 permanent ones. The highway patrol served some 18,000 disabled cars. Members of the Speaker's Bureau delivered 276 addresses, and the official Hotel and Garage Department investigated 758 complaints.

Traffic accidents continued to disturb the Club. While auto registration had gone up 7 percent during the first seven months of 1929, auto deaths had increased 35 percent. Tourist traffic, too, continued to leap, a 30 percent increase over the past year with some 97,236 autos checking into the Southland with 2,680,597 visitors to the state. Seven million motorists visited national parks in California during the same period.

PLATE *19* *The Pacific Coast Highway above Santa Monica, August, 1925.*

Fledgling groups were now turning to the Club for aid. One was the Arizona Automobile Association. Mired in the sands of financial woes, the Arizona group asked the Club for the loan of a jack. C. E. McStay, a Club troubleshooter, was sent. The problem: the Arizona club was called upon to help an inordinate number of non-resident motorists traveling through the state. Quite obviously, with southern California their destination, this area had a stake in seeing they got here. McStay set out on a program of twenty-three meetings with prominent citizens of Arizona to convince them of the importance of highway travel. By building up the membership of the Arizona club the hurdle was surmounted.

The American Automobile Association continued to fight for a foothold in southern California, trying to establish branches. The break of 1915 had never been mended. The AAA was particularly concerned about the Club policy of serving all out-of-state motorists as guests without charge. Too, it seemed to Club directors the AAA was interested only in benefiting from the Club's services while offering nothing in return. The Club, after a complicated exchange, wrote the AAA, frankly expressing these feelings.

The Interinsurance Exchange, first organized in 1912, was keeping pace with the burgeoning membership. But it faced one clear competitive problem despite its steady growth. Many members who wanted to have their insurance with the Exchange, couldn't, for the simple reason that auto dealers required them to take insurance with companies of the dealer's choice, if the car was financed by the dealer. The problem had been with the Club for years, but in 1925, a solution of sorts had been found. The Club entered into a contract with the Faye Securities Co., an auto financing firm, with the understanding that members could finance their new autos with the finance firm and the exchange would handle the insurance. The program worked for several years. But there were difficulties—difficulties that were not the fault of either agency. In 1928, a study was started to find another solution, and the following year a report by a special committee suggested that a Club finance department be organized. It was approved.

Meanwhile, an insidious pattern was taking shape on Wall Street. The stock market broke in September, 1929, but quickly recovered, then slipped again. Some investors were hurt, but there was little real alarm until October 21. Havoc reigned with panic selling, and total demoralization came October 28. By November 13, it was all over—Coolidge Prosperity, the carefree spending, the paper millionaires, the Big Bull Market.

As a shattered nation tried to pick up the pieces, blame was placed. There had been overproduction, artificial commodity prices, a silver price collapse, an international financial derangement due to shifting gold, unrest in foreign lands and "psychological reactions."

It all made little difference. For the Great Depression was upon us. With it came serious problems and needs for adjustments and changes within the Club. A crisis was here.

Chapter 9

EMPTY WALLET BLUES

"Wall Street may sell stocks, but Main Street is still buying goods."

—Newspaper advertisement, 1930

THE DEPRESSION came—first with a bang, then with a whimper. Wall Street, stunned and devastated as it was, waited for a "readjustment." President Hoover felt sure things would return to "normalcy" again. Businessmen—confused, grim, but still optimistic—sat back waiting for that magic moment when the economy would "turn the corner." People would buy their way back to prosperity again.

The Club was caught up in this curious hesitation in 1930. It was in excellent condition, like a young heavyweight at his prime. In the previous fifteen years, membership had soared from a modest 6,500 to 136,392. It had expanded with branch offices, new services and new departments. There was money in the bank. Club directors were among the most influential and astute business leaders in Los Angeles, and the bustling staff was a study in energy, creativity and aggressiveness.

As for the southern Californian, he was established in an affluent way of life. Wall Street was far away. "It will all blow over," was the common attitude, despite some dire and solemn economic prognostications.

There were plenty of new diversions. That rival competitor in oranges and tourism, Florida, had spawned the new game of miniature golf, and there was soon a $125-million boom across the U.S.—with everyone knocking balls through tiny windmills and into disguised drainpipes. Soon after came driving ranges. Bobby Jones was the subject of endless talk, as were the latest escapades of Amos 'n' Andy. Tree-sitting was the concern of the day's young eccentrics, along with marathon dancing. And a new wonder came that year with the latest autos, called "free-wheeling." Talk swirled, like a fresh batch of bathtub gin, over whether pulling a lever on the dashboard *really* saved gas and how it *really* affected the motor.

Autos had evolved into solid, boxlike affairs. Earlier, cursory attempts at streamlining had generally gone by the board. The Chrysler of 1930 (town sedan, $1,295) emphasized such mechanical marvels as a seven-bearing, counter-weighted crankshaft, rubber spring shackles and adjustable front seats. The Plymouth with dressy fender welds could be had for $655, while the luxurious Dusenberg convertible sedan boasted wire wheels and 265 horsepower. Another similar luxury item was the Marmon ("under $5,000"), while in the middle-priced range were such standbys as the

LaSalle, a Cadillac offering and the Cord Front Drive, produced by Auburn. By April 14, 1931, the 20 millionth Ford, a black Model-A sedan, was touring the country on a promotional trip but creating none of the furor of the first Model-A. Reverse snobbism had set in by now, and Nash proudly advertised its product as "a new style . . . not from Paris but from Nash."

In Europe, a curious automotive misadventure ended in chaos that year. Ettore Bugatti, the king of racing cars, was infuriated by a wealthy matron who remarked over her soufflé that his racers were nice enough, but for a decent town car the Rolls-Royce remained the only respectable means of transportation. Thus challenged, he set out to produce the most expensive and finest passenger auto the world had ever known for the $30,000-and-up market. La Royale, as he crowned his wonder, went into production with twenty-five chassis ordered. It had a wheelbase of over fourteen feet and was a straight eight with 784 cubic inches (twice today's Cadillac). Every working part of the vehicle was honed to tolerance zero. It boasted four button horns, one for each steering wheel spoke, and the hood was seven feet long, with an ivory elephant radiator ornament. Minimum price to buyers was $40,000, and that was just for the near affluent. The Depression ended the noble dream. Only seven La Royales were produced, King Alfonso of Spain buying one, King Carol of Rumania another.

The Club wasn't concerned with such extravagances, however. A Rolls-Royce was still relatively unknown in the West; Fords, Chevrolets, Plymouths and Buicks were the concern.

Business was bustling, and despite the ominous predictions by the city slickers of the Eastern seaboard, it was generally decided that the country would pull out of the slump.

Indeed, in January, 1930, the directors authorized a building program to double the size of Club headquarters; it was bursting at the seams. Cost totaled $1,127,555.

The arrangement to finance members' autos through Faye Securities Co. had turned out badly, through no fault of either party. The problem was a recurring bugaboo for the Club. Dealers and finance companies were charging high rates of interest and demanding insurance be placed with carriers of their choice. The Club, through its Exchange, refused to cooperate with them, seeking another way to give low-interest financing and also the Exchange's low insurance rates. A study finally convinced directors that the Club had to do this itself. On July 1, 1930, the finance department started with a conservative policy at 6 percent on new passenger autos (which was to be later lowered to 4½ percent in 1935 and 4 percent in 1946) which also allowed members to buy insurance through the Club. Today it remains a constant attraction for new members.

The American public sat back mildly puzzled and hesitant in those months after the Crash. President Hoover worried as his prestige dropped, but he issued optimistic predictions. World affairs—the London Arms Conference, for example—led to an unexpectedly brutal tariff bill by Congress which hurt the economic situation even more. Trying to sustain cotton and wheat prices was difficult enough. When a drought hit the East, it made matters worse.

The Club, like thousands of other enterprises across the land, waited for the long-promised change. It came. But the change was down and down and down. In June, 1930, membership was then at an all-time high of 137,698. Now the cutbacks, the dropouts began to show. Six months later some 3,000 memberships had disappeared. It went steadily down. On December 31, 1931, there were 125,778 members, and 23,-000 more memberships were gone a year later. It continued down until the worried directors were to look disconsolately at a roll of only 81,202, representing a loss of some 55,000 in four years.

Still, the end was not yet. The low point was to come May 30, 1934, with only approximately 77,000 members, a decrease of some 40 percent since the Club's heyday in 1929. Happily, this was the bottom, as later records indicate a slow growth. An accurate count is difficult during this entire era since minutes do not distinguish among actual members and memberships collectible or paid-up. It was to be August, 1941, however, before membership passed the old peak of 1929.

The losses in membership revenue of $720,000 per annum during the low period was to have a snowballing effect on other revenues. The Interinsurance Exchange naturally had fewer policies, and there was danger of complete collapse of the Standard Accident Insurance Company with its liability insurance policy loss. Since the Club acted as a broker, and received a commission for placement of members' policies here, more losses were sustained.

Facing directors during this horrendous era was the age-old nemesis—

balancing the budget. By January, 1932, a variety of steps had to be taken. There was a cutback in the number of patrol cars and a reduction in city salesmen and branch employees. Sick benefits and mileage allowance were revised, along with a general cutback of 7½ percent in salaries. Three months later, Club Secretary Standish L. Mitchell sadly reported seventy-two employees had been dismissed and that, by restricting vacations, some $141,000 in expenses would be saved that year.

In December of that year, the directors took a look at the proposed budget for 1933. There was ahead a further drop in income of 16.6 percent, Carl E. McStay told them. The directors decided on a general policy on releasing employees. Only those whose jobs were absolutely nonessential would be laid off, and unneeded women employees with working husbands would go first.

Meanwhile, aggressive efforts to attract new members were tried. A radio and newspaper advertising campaign was started. The Club matched $25,000 with a like amount from the Exchange in the try. Yet, there was a steady whittling away of the membership. The yearly enrollment fee was dropped from $5.00 to $3.00. Management visited branch offices regularly to encourage employees and members to submit names of prospective members. This marked the beginning of the Gold Emblem Honor Roll which continued for some years. Posters in official garages and sales pamphlets for new members were spread throughout southern California.

Despite the prevailing air of fear and concern during these difficult years when some 11 million Americans were without jobs, Club activities continued to maintain and build what had been created over the previous three decades.

Early in 1930, a report shows the Broken Glass Patrol car had removed 497 heaps of broken glass from roads during the previous November. The hotel department placed 834 reservations for members that same month, and excavation was started for the annex to the Club building at Adams and Figueroa. On New Year's Day, 1930, the Club aided the Rose Parade by erecting 3,000 temporary road signs and by distributing special route maps while the Map Department issued a new index map of the western states.

The unhappy relations with the American Automobile Association continued. The Club received word in 1930 that the AAA planned another foray into southern California and had authorized the establishment of a division in the area. Club directors were not too disturbed; the Club was already adequately serving both nonresident tourists, and AAA members as well, in this area. But the California State Automobile Association wrote the AAA stating that it would refuse to recognize the proposed AAA division and would continue to deal with the Automobile Club of Southern California.

Road-charting and sign-posting went on at a lively pace. In April, 1930, the Touring Bureau crews covered some 7,000 miles, and the sign-posting department reported it had placed more thant 200,000 signs in southern California. In June, the sign-posting scout cars and trucks covered 22,000 miles, erecting 1,000 new signs and painting 6,562 posts. The emergency service in November, 1930, reported a typical month. It answered 5,657 calls, which included 1,517 flat tires, 937 autos with ignition trouble, 1,344 with starter or battery woes and 391 with burned-out bearings. Collision and other mishap accounted for 563 more.

Legislative activity continued strong. The Club opposed a proposal to finance the San Francisco Bay bridges out of either the state general fund or the state highway fund. It also opposed a gas tax increase to four cents and an increase of the vehicle license fee. Too, the Club stood pat against various measures to use the state general fund to aid joint highway districts and compulsory insurance. The fight against the efforts of northern California interests to get highway money at Southland expense went on. At the time, the north had 69 percent of the state highway mileage and southern California had only 31 percent, even though the latter had 48 percent of the state's area, 55 percent of the taxable wealth, 59 percent of the registered vehicles and 55 percent of the population. The state had its own explanation for all this. State Highway Engineer C. H. Purcell explained to the Club that it was impossible to divide funds each year exactly as the allocation act required. He went on to explain that many budgeted projects in southern California had been held up by the problems of obtaining right-of-way.

The Club was still involved in adventures—some of an intensely exciting nature. The International Pacific Highway Caravan, an elaborately planned venture to southern Mexico, took off in 1930 in support of constructing an international road from Alaska to Mexico and on into South America. The caravan averaged—after thirty days—1.6 miles per day. In one seventeen-mile section the Tehuantepec River had to be forded eighty-

PLATES *20 and 21 Gashing a path through Mexico for the International Pacific Highway was a gargantuan task. Here, the sixty-sixth of more than eighty fordings of the Rio Tehuantepec, and dynamite blasting south of Nejapa.*

eight times. If all went well, the expedition was to reach Tehuantepec, 568 miles south of Mexico City in about six days, directors were informed, at one point. The expedition was successful, and the Club proved that an international highway along the Pacific Coast of Western Hemisphere countries was feasible—though its actual construction was to be realized many years later.

Harry J. Bauer, who had had a long career with the Club and had been a director since 1926, was reelected president about the same time. In his annual report, he commented on the now-occupied addition to the Club structure, on five new branch offices completed and three more under construction, and on the formation of the Finance Department.

Although the greatest crisis of the Depression was yet to come, one can sense the nervous concern of the time, despite the cheery face put on by civic leaders. Anxious to encourage tourist dollars, the state Chamber of Commerce, California Newspaper Publishers Association and others created a Fiesta Year in which the Club and many other civic groups were lively participants. Some 169 towns put on nearly 400 fetes to lure visitors in the year of 1931.

Meanwhile, happy news came from the highway commission. It agreed to restore to southern California by future contract the $962,000 which, in the recent past, had been expended in the north.

Despite quarrels, highways were being built nearly everywhere. In 1911 there had been somewhere between 500 and 1,000 miles of road which could be termed serviceable. Now, twenty years later, there were 25,000 miles. "Today the 154-mile trip from Hollywood to Tijuana can be made in less than six hours," it was proclaimed.

Progress, though tedious and slow, was still evident. The Finance Department proudly claimed only four autos had been repossessed at a loss of $353.29 and that 1,613 contracts had been issued. Yet, some efforts misfired. The directors endorsed a suggestion by Director Harry Chandler to build an aerial tramway to Glacier Point in the Yosemite Park. But opposition developed, and the project failed.

The subtle, numbing effects of joblessness were being felt. County supervisors had proposed that a state bond issue for $20 million and a one-cent increase in the gas tax be arranged to assist the unemployed. The Club's directors opposed the idea as still another effort to raid the gas tax for other than highway purposes.

Pressures were also being felt within the Club by now. The first eight months of 1931 showed a decline of new membership sales of 1,826, and the withdrawals were 4,026 more than for the same period in 1930. Hopes that the economy would soon turn the corner were disappearing everywhere. Directors, in the fall of 1931, reluctantly voted to forego the

PLATE *22 The pathfinders pose just before their departure for Panama, March 15, 1930, on the first of the Club-sponsored Pacific Highway expeditions to search for a road route from Los Angeles to Central America.*

usual Christmas check to employees equal to 15 percent of one month's salary. By the end of the year, a variety of other dollar-saving devices were taking shape. The custom of sending personal notices of the annual meeting to each member of the Club was discontinued. The idea of cutting working hours and adjusting salaries downward when absolutely necessary was discussed.

As directors faced up to the prospects of 1932, they saw only gloom. The Secretary presented a report which caught the dismal prospects ahead: during 1931 the income of the Club fell $165,000 below the 1930 income. Economies had been made effective to reduce the operating cost $225,500 below that of 1930. "However, in January, 1932 there is a carry over deficit of $30,000. We expect 1932 to be no better, possibly worse. Thus, the proposed budget for 1932 is cut $215,000 below 1931 expenditures. . . ."

The nation was magnificently bewildered in December, 1931, twenty-six months after the Crash. Peter F. Drucker noted: "Depression shows a man as a senseless cog in a senselessly whirling machine which is beyond human understanding and has ceased to serve any purpose but its own."

As for those ceaselessly whirling machines in the United States—the autos—obvious things happened. People walked. People didn't buy new cars. People didn't take the Sunday drive. People didn't take long trips.

In June of that year, two New York State politicians, Governor Franklin D. Roosevelt and James A. Farley, mulled over plans for an approaching trip by Farley to Seattle to attend an Elks' convention. The plot: Farley was to stop along the way across country to feel out political sentiment concerning the nomination of Roosevelt on the Democratic ticket for the presidency. About the same time the incumbent president, Herbert Hoover, decided waiting for readjustment wasn't enough. He began an offensive in international finance to change things. Despite valiant efforts, however, the Depression was to worsen.

The Club directors had been right in their cheerless prediction that the most brutal times were yet to come. For the year 1932 was to be rock bottom.

SPECIAL PICTURE SECTION

Six Decades of Motoring in Southern California

PLATE *23 Auto Pioneer Earle C. Anthony, at age 17, built in 1897 this vehicle with buckboards and bicycle wheels, using a chain drive and electric motor which he also built himself.*

PLATE *24 In 1893 the standard means of public transportation in Los Angeles was the horse-drawn car such as the Main Street special which ran to the Redondo Beach depot.* (Historical Collections Security First National Bank)

110

PLATE 25 *The first auto in Los Angeles was built by E. E. Erie, a local, in 1887. In the rear seat is a city father, William H. Workman.* (Historical Collections Security First National Bank)

PLATE 26 *They said it couldn't be done, but in Pasadena, 1903, tinkerers were still seeking a practical answer to cheap transportation.* (Title Insurance and Trust Company [Los Angeles] Collection of Historical Photographs)

PLATE 27 *The Mobile Stanhope Steamer of 1900 was an oddity on Hollywood Boulevard. The driver is General Sherman of the Pacific Electric Railroad and his crony, Los Angeles Sheriff William A. Hammel.* (Title Insurance and Trust Company [Los Angeles] Collection of Historical Photographs)

PLATE 28 *Probably a Woods Electric, about 1900. The dandy is pictured wistfully awaiting a lady on a Sunday afternoon.* (Title Insurance and Trust Company [Los Angeles] Collection of Historical Photographs)

112

PLATE *29* *The "Tourist" was one of the few autos manufactured in Los Angeles. It had a brief career for two years.* (Historical Collections Security First National Bank)

PLATE *30* *A bevy of adventurous motorists often made forays to rural areas. Here vehicles rest while merrymaking goes on at the ranch house.* (Historical Collections Security First National Bank)

PLATE *31 In 1903 the ladies didn't drive the automobiles. But they loved to pose on them.* (Historical Collections Security First National Bank)

PLATE *32 In 1904 Los Angeles' Mounted Police were heroic figures when they spun down Broadway in formation.* (Title Insurance and Trust Company [Los Angeles] Collection of Historical Photographs)

PLATE *33* *The cluster of Los Angeles' curbstone sophisticates on the left were already bored by autos by 1905. They are clustered around the entrance of the Hotel Berwick, which offered massage and baths and who knows what other forgotten sins.* (Title Insurance and Trust Company [Los Angeles] Collection of Historical Photographs)

PLATE *34* *She's a 1905 Cadillac, a wondrous toy of the day—but even such expensive luxuries had spasms and pains constantly.* (Historical Collections Security First National Bank)

PLATE *35* *A Los Angeles Auto Club tour in 1904 along Sunset Boulevard brought out motordom's best and bravest.* (Title Insurance and Trust Company [Los Angeles] Collection of Historical Photographs)

PLATE *36* *In 1905 such rakes as the man in the electric* (foreground) *risked jibes and indignation when they ventured downtown.* (Title Insurance and Trust Company [Los Angeles] Collection of Historical Photographs)

PLATE 37 *A White Steamer comes across bad times in Santa Cruz in 1906. The rural in the background is even more firmly convinced that the city dandies with their infernal machines are crazy.*

PLATE 38 *The 1907 Ford was a study in classic utility.* (Historical Collections Security First National Bank)

PLATE *39* *The Newhall Pass of 1906 called for crafty steering. A White Steamer pauses to seek photographic immortality.*

PLATE 40 *What price glory? Well, how about riding in the 1909 Elks Parade in Los Angeles to help the Orphans' Fund in a Packard decorated with 11,000 lavender Centaureas? It won the $250 first prize.*

PLATE 41 *One of the inevitable hazards of the road. A dashing rascal in striped blazer has to take time off to repair a tire.* (Historical Collections Security First National Bank)

PLATE *42 The 1903 Reliability Race from Los Angeles to the Palomares Hotel in Pomona wiped out many of the contestants. Here are the proud winners and admirers.*

PLATE *43 This 1900 Stanley Steamer was the first car into Yosemite, a yeoman's feat in tricky driving.*

PLATE *44* *Who but the most jaded and worldly of 1907 would not pause for a photograph as he passed under the Wawona Big Tree?*

122

PLATE 45   *A party of funsters in a White Steamer pause along the Monterey Peninsula in 1906 to gather sea shells by the seashore.*

PLATE 46   *Among the wild but possible adventures of 1906 was exploring the Santa Susana Grade, an uncharted wilderness of elfin forest.*

PLATE 47 *In the days of the Model-T* (background), *a pioneer poses with what was already a vintage model.* (Historical Collections Security First National Bank)

PLATE 48 *Gay caballeros prepare to ride in* La Fiesta de Los Angeles *about 1910, mounts courtesy of the city's street-cleaning department.* (Title Insurance and Trust Company [Los Angeles] Collection of Historical Photographs)

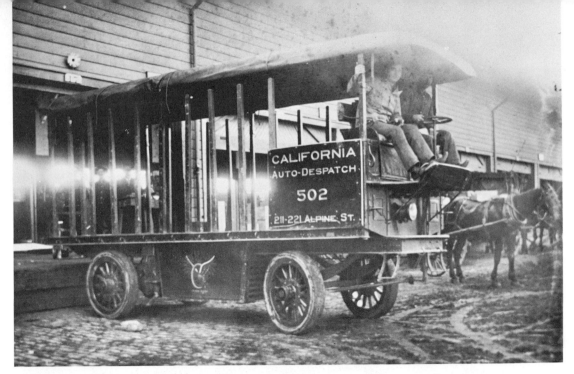

PLATE 49 *Two draymen pose on one of the first trucks before setting out on a "despatch."* (Historical Collections Security First National Bank)

PLATE 50 *One of Los Angeles' more affluent citizens poses near Pershing Square before World War I.* (Historical Collections Security First National Bank)

PLATE *51* *Elysian Park was one of Los Angeles' major playgrounds about 1910. A group of rounders pose before touring the semi-tropical wonderland.* (Historical Collections Security First National Bank)

PLATE *52* *In Pasadena, where things tend to be conservative, chariot racing was the fashionable new fad in 1911.* (Title Insurance and Trust Company [Los Angeles] Collection of Historical Photographs)

PLATE *53 By 1910 the auto was still an oddity and plaything in Los Angeles. The buggy still held sway.* (Title Insurance and Trust Company [Los Angeles] Collection of Historical Photographs)

PLATE 54   *In downtown Los Angeles, 1915, the problem of parking was a minor crisis even during afternoon rush hour.* (Title Insurance and Trust Company [Los Angeles] Collection of Historical Photographs)

PLATE 55 *Bicycles and automobiles were both offered by dealers in 1910, with the more reliant bike getting top billing. The shop was near Fifth and Spring streets, Los Angeles.* (Title Insurance and Trust Company [Los Angeles] Collection of Historical Photographs)

PLATE 56 *About the time Columbus set forth, a latter-day Nostradamus, one Mother Shipton, predicted the future of mankind. Here is an anti-auto artist's rendition of the truth of her prophecy.* (Title Insurance and Trust Company [Los Angeles] Collection of Historical Photographs)

Carriages without horses shall go,
And accidents fill the world with woe.

Old Mother Shipton has been vindicated insofar as this part of her prophecy is concerned. Of course, it is now generally believed that the verse, of which the foregoing is only a part, was a hoax to the extent that the predictions were circulated after most of the predicted things had come to pass.

But it must be admitted that the author of the introductory lines anticipated present-day traffic problems. The comic sketch here shown appeared in 1828 shortly after the advent of steam carriages which was nearly four centuries after Mother Shipton is supposed to have lived. The artist was himself something of a seer because he attempted to show how the streets would some day be clogged by horseless carriages.

PLATE 57   *In 1916 the Club initiated the "travelling garage" with trained mechanics. The service was a wild success. The scene is the Tioga Road.*

PLATE 58   *The Club's posting of El Camino Real with mission bells was a highlight. Tourists pause near Capistrano to view the new refinement in motoring.*

PLATE 59 *The 1914 sign-posting trip across the U.S. was made by this sturdy craft seen passing over one of the better bridges of the interior.*

PLATE 60 *In 1910 White Water Point was the great barrier for the auto driver. A crafty operator with mules stood by and charged a fee to haul adventurers out of the sand.*

PLATE 61 *Famed racing driver Ralph de Palma chugs home to victory in a road race before World War I.*

PLATE *62*   *How about a nice Sunday drive to Ventura? This was the road in 1916.*

PLATE *63*   *The devious sands of Palm Springs were a major challenge in 1911 for derring-do motorists. Breakdown was part of the game.*

132

PLATE 64   One of the many sign-posting expeditions by the Club. The driver pauses near Pueblo, Colorado, in May, 1917.

PLATE 65   When six Sioux chiefs visited Los Angeles in the 1920s, they were given a grand city tour by Pacific Electric. (Historical Collections Security First National Bank)

PLATE 66 *A collection of early autos. In line: a 1907 Cadillac; a 1905 Stevens-Duryea; a 1903 White; a hybrid of uncertain parentage; a 1907 Firestone Buggymobile.* (Historical Collections Security First National Bank)

PLATE 67 *By the early 1920s downtown Los Angeles was taking on the look of today's traffic-heavy rush.* (Title Insurance and Trust Company [Los Angeles] Collection of Historical Photographs)

PLATE 68 *In the 1920s the flappers and rakes sometimes cut up touches in old autos such as this aging Cadillac.* (Historical Collections Security First National Bank)

PLATE 69 *In 1921 a Pony Express run through the desert wilderness was a merry stunt. The crew above spins through the sands near Blythe.*

PLATE 70 *Showing the old and the new has always been a national hobby in the auto business. Here an enterprising dealer tries to lure customers with his newest phaeton.* (Historical Collections Security First National Bank)

PLATE 71 *In 1925 the coast near Los Angeles was still an almost empty paradise for the bather and clam digger.*

PLATE 72 *By 1950 Angelenos had found the glories of sun basking and surfing.*

PLATE 73 *The 1924 Highway Patrol Service was growing and the proud white wagon was a happy sign for the distressed motorist.*

PLATE *74* *The Ridge Route between Bakersfield and Los Angeles was a rich emotional experience back in 1927.*

PLATE 75 *By 1928 the Club's Highway Patrol Service sported fancy uniforms.*

PLATE 76 *"Gadzooks!" shouted such outraged pedestrians as this citizen in the mid-dle of Spring Street in Los Angeles, 1927.* (Title Insurance and Trust Company [Los Angeles] Collection of Historical Photographs)

PLATE 77 *The day when aviation became a stern reality was a nervous time for the Club. The compass diagram on the roof was a friendly aid in 1928 to passing biplanes headed north.*

PLATE 78 *The greatest excitement in the history of motordom came with the first showing of Henry Ford's Model-A, which caused riots in the East. This is a 1931 model.*

PLATE 79 *In 1931 the Auto Club set out to chart passage through the state of Chiapas in Mexico for the highway through Central America. The drivers pause in San Felipe.*

PLATE *80* *Getting over the donkey trails was an adventurous task in 1930. Peons help tug the exploration auto for the International-American Highway over a rough spot in the interior of Mexico.*

PLATE *81   In 1941 the Club sponsored the Give them a Lift program for the military.*

PLATE *82   The massive earthmovers rumbled through the Sepulveda ravine in 1962, ripping the way for the freeway.*

PLATE *83   The proverbial far cry from the day of the stalled tourist who could expect limitless problems and delay is today's Club service which tries to be on the
scene of crisis in twenty minutes.*

PLATE *84   Today the crumbling remains of the old plank road in the Imperial Valley can still be seen.*

PLATE 85 *One of the sad but inevitable consequences of the motoring age, the litter-bug.*

PLATE 86 *Ribbons of concrete ornament in Los Angeles. The Santa Monica Harbor Interchange, 1962.*

146

Chapter 10

THE SPARE TIRE IS THIN

"Franklin D. Roosevelt is no crusader. He is no tribune of the people. He is no enemy of entrenched privilege. He is a pleasant man who, without any important qualifications for the office, would very much like to be President."

—Walter Lippmann
New York *Herald-Tribune*, 1931

IF THE prediction of the widely respected Lippmann was slightly off base in the beginning of the 1930s, so was the prediction of nearly everyone else. President Hoover had called for confidence and optimism to a vast army of disbelievers. The Rev. Norman Vincent Peale had his own solution, "a good prayer meeting on Wall Street." Everywhere the mirage of hope and inspiration was sold as one of the few commercial commodities anyone would buy. Magazines and movies were full of radiant good cheer. Wily John Nance Garner plugged the Democratic idea that the Depression was a wholly owned subsidiary of the Republican Party, even when FDR, after he took office, continued the refrain that cheery days were still "just around the corner."

Escape was the order of the day. One such device was 3.2 beer, which President Roosevelt had installed as part of his political program. Amos 'n' Andy, Jack Benny, Fred Allen had all offered brief moments for momentary withdrawal. But everywhere were shack towns, and the ubiquitous old rattletrap Model-T or Franklin filled with disenfranchised Dust Bowl refugees crowded the roads of California.

Everyone had an answer, simplistic as it might be. A variety of kookie cults based on strange economic doctrines popped up in southern California. In exclusive clubs in the East the disenchanted invented new jokes about the Roosevelts, while in Washington, D.C. press agents mimeographed tirades attacking the "economic royalists" who wouldn't allow the country to get back on its feet. Townsendites and Technocrats had their theories and answers, as did Father Divine and Huey Long.

A best-selling book of the time, *Oh Yeah,* caught the cynical flavor of those first grim years. It was filled with the prophecies of the important statesmen and powerful bankers, all glib and cheerful predictions coming at the onset of the Depression.

Yet, the beginning of 1932 was numbing in its cold fury. The average number of unemployed people in the country was 12.5 million according to the National Industrial Conference Board, over 13 million according to the American Federation of Labor and—by other estimates—anywhere from 8 to 17 million. As for money paid out in 1932 salaries: about 40 percent less went out in payrolls; dividends dropped 56.6 percent; wages went down 60 percent. Existing businesses tried to hang on. Almost no new businesses started. In the large cities hundreds of shops were vacant and dusty. There weren't the trucks on the streets there had once been. (Yet, paradoxically, the filling station was one of the few retail business categories which seemed to stay even. Less new autos were bought, but the old ones were pressed to more and more uses as train travel declined.)

A lot of automotive events had transpired by 1931. The "firsts" of a quarter century before—the first truck to haul beer barrels, the first rumble seat, the Cleveland ordinance for police to stop firing at the tires of speeding autos—were all ancient history. Wild innovations, such as the Gale tilting body of 1906, which allowed owners to simply lift the car body up rather than crawl under the vehicle, and "pneumatic bumperettes," had come and gone.

The autos of 1931 were in mood with the times, solemn and square. The Chrysler straight eight (coupe with rumble seat, $1,495) stressed safety and silence. Overhead valve gears were a subject for debate. Raven black was fittingly enough the popular hue, touched with just the beginnings of chromium trim. Trade names now vanished were still about—the Franklin, Cunningham, Cord, Marmon. The de-Vaux Six made a brief, brave bid in the low-priced field (phaeton, $545), offering a V-shaped radiator shield, L-head engine, 65 horsepower.

But it didn't really make a lot of difference. The self-indulgent delight of arguing over what new car to buy was something few Americans could longer enjoy. "Make do" was the order of the day. From all signs, business was destined to get worse. Everywhere executives sat down to puzzle over ways of keeping their enterprises afloat. Too, millions of jobless sat in another strange manifestation of the times. Most of them had tried pounding the sidewalks in the search for that evasive oddity, a "Help Wanted" sign. Now they sat listlessly and with vacant stares. They had just given up.

Club directors were convinced that 1932 was to be an even unhappier year than the previous one. The first week of that year a conference was held. Attending were the chairman of the finance committee, Horace G. Miller, the executive committee chairman, W. L. Valentine, President Harry Bauer and staffers. Mission: to decide upon operating expenses.

Reserves were still ample. But the real squeeze was on. It was decided the Interinsurance Exchange should cut back on employees and salaries just as the Club had already done.

Meanwhile, outside business continued. The directors continued to oppose a proposed federal gas tax and automobile tax, adopted a resolution calling for a garage to be included in the new Los Angeles Federal building soon to be constructed, and mulled over the implications of the bankruptcy of the Automobile Club of America in New York.

Touring had, surprisingly, touched new horizons—perhaps because of the Depression. Distribution of the Club guidebook covering auto routes from Mexico City to British Columbia had totaled 30,000 copies in two years. Canadian authorities were also pushing an aerial survey of the highway on to Alaska, another 1,400 miles, with plans for it to extend from Hazelton, British Columbia.

The annual report, issued in March, 1932, showed the generally sad picture. It recited, primarily, money-saving devices which had been put in effect, noted that membership had dropped to 125,776, a 6.7 percent decline.

The need for money was apparent in every action and counter-action by now. The Club fought a move by Congress once again to impose an excise tax on automobile manufacture. Too, it stood against proposed legislation by the county requiring presentation of a certificate of assessment before annual renewal of motor vehicle registration. The Club directed Allen Davis, Chief Legal Counsel, to negotiate and work out a plan which would put a minimum burden on auto owners.

The fight also continued over equitable distribution of funds between north and south for highways. A meeting in June served as the foundation for legislation to come in 1933, and was a major victory for southern California in this perennial controversy. A meeting a few months later between the California State Automobile Association and the Club was helpful when the two groups agreed on twelve points, including the concept of adding 2,900 miles of highway in the north and 3,724 miles in the south. This was to equalize the secondary miles at 4,848 in each area and to follow the basic principles of the Breed Bill, with some minor changes to bring areas into balance and relieve county taxpayers.

But the constant decline in income made such progress difficult. By November 28, 1932, the gross membership had gone down to 104,803, a loss of 16.6 percent, or nearly 21,000 during the year. Yet, other auto clubs across the land were faring as badly—or even worse. The California State Automobile Association reported a drop of 13.3 percent for the same period, while Chicago had dropped 21.3 percent, Michigan 12.5 percent. The average for twenty-five of the leading American Automobile Association clubs was 19.4 percent. (The U. S. Chambers of Commerce charted the general tenor of business for the period by reporting a 25 percent drop in memberships in chambers of commerce throughout the U.S.)

While worried directors pondered answers, the membership continued to decline as the full impact of the Depression hit the economy. By February, 1933, paid-up membership was 81,402, with 8,402 collectible memberships in arrears. Moreover, subtle influences engendered by the financial plight cast their shadows over Club activities. Typical was a problem in the insurance bureau. It had been Club policy until 1929 to have more than one casualty company on hand to place liability insurance. For various reasons, Standard Accident Insurance Company then started receiving all such insurance. But this company had been forced to discontinue certain bad risks among Club members, despite its most satisfactory general service to the Club. It, like all such firms, had gone through a decline in market value of its securities. Directors decided the Club's first duty was to its membership in protecting them, and they sought out another firm to carry part of the liability line.

As if the chaotic state of economics were not enough, nature took a hand in more tragic events for 1933. An earthquake struck the Long Beach area. The Club suffered its share of loss. The Huntington Park office was so badly shattered it was unfit for occupancy, and the Compton sub-office was a total wreck. In Long Beach and Inglewood, both Club offices were damaged, but still usable. Within two hours after the quake, five Club patrol cars had been on the job in the stricken area, busy with relief work. Later, fifty-two claims totaling $2,866.99 were filed by members whose autos were damaged in the catastrophe.

Even while fighting off calamity occupied a major proportion of the directors' time, they continued in some aggressive moves for more revenue —even though the dollars were scarce for such activities.

How to push for new membership and keep Club activities before the public at minimum cost, for example? Everyone was struggling desperately for business. It was quite natural that the California Newspaper Publishers Association complained that the Club was spending too much of its advertising budget on radio programs. After all, it asked, hadn't the state's newspapers published Club news for years? Only to have the Club begin advertising on radio.

Directors, however, had the Club's welfare to consider. The cost for fifty-one radio programs in seventeen weeks with sixteen minutes to each program, including a minute devoted to promoting the Club's money-saving services, was the same as a single full-page ad in some fifty of southern California's dailies.

While this facet of advertising was one concern, getting added revenue from *Touring Topics* was another. The question of accepting beer and wine advertising was discussed. But the prohibition atmosphere still lingered. Directors were fearful of indignant reader response, despite the explanation by Director Harry Chandler, publisher of the Los Angeles *Times,* that his paper had quit advertising hard liquor because of complaints, but continued to advertise wine and beer because subscribers didn't seem to object. Yet the directors—anxious as they were for added revenue —decided to hold off.

The National Recovery Act was put into effect that year and the directors voted for the Club to qualify by signing the pledge. The Club and Exchange plan called for a thirty-five-hour week for employees who were mechanics or artisans, and a forty-hour week for office workers with an eight-hour day, and no salary decrease. Excepted were certain skilled technicians, salesmen on the road and executives.

At the same time an advertising program was approved, with a $50,000 budget for the year, half of which was to be spent on radio and a special supplement of *Touring Topics,* the other half for newspaper advertising. It was at the same time that it became apparent *Touring Topics* had to emerge as a more important publication. The late Phil Townsend Hanna, Editor, called for a drive to increase circulation and seek more advertising, as well as to change the name of the magazine. In the fast-paced world of motordom, the old name had a slightly archaic sound. "Touring" was in the past—the auto was now a standard fixture in everyday American life.

And, despite the dire times, men of vision still dreamed. Director Harry Chandler convinced United Press it should pay heed to the idea of building the International Pacific Highway, to reach the length of South America. UP borrowed the films of the Club's two caravan trips to do stories that were to reach some 400 U.S. newspapers.

Meanwhile, the search for a new name for *Touring Topics* was a lively Club event of 1933. Members had time to mull over the matter and hundreds of suggestions were submitted. The Board finally announced eight-seven new names that seemed likely candidates for subcommitte consideration. The problem as the directors saw it: to select a name broad enough in scope that would validly cover all subjects of interest to motorists, but still not disassociate itself from the Club. The directors voted on the suggested names. "WESTWAYS" won, with "Tides West" in second place and "El Dorado" selected as third.

But the economic gloom was constant. A clue to the concern can be found in the report of the manager of the Exchange, who visited seven district offices to get a feel of the climate. His conclusion: district managers were of the theory that business had not yet reached rock bottom—there was more bad news to come. They did note one cheery factor, however. The loss of business in November, 1933, had not been as great as anticipated when the year's budget had been made.

If the whole climate was one of cost-cutting during those tight years, it was to have its good effect. One major concern had been the complications of function between county and state agencies in matters of highways. In February, 1934, a progress report on street and highway administration was presented to Club directors. It compared mileage of state, county and city roads as well as their administration and financing. The study looked at the state highway department and compared it with the fifty-eight boards of supervisors in the state. The results were not flattering to the counties.

It was clear the state highway department was much more efficient, while there was a never-ending parade of changing personnel in the county offices. Individual political control in the counties also worked havoc in the appropriation expenditures. County funds, it was noted, were divided into five equal parts for no real reason. Such a method led to duplication in road machinery and almost impossible barriers in developing coordinated county main highways into an integrated system. It seemed clear from the report that all county highways should be administered by one central state authority. Club directors adopted a resolution calling for such an authority and directing the Club's engineering and legal departments to go to work preparing detailed plans for such a program.

It was a matter of stomping where the proverbial angels fear to tread. Local politics were deeply involved in such matters, and wresting such funds from them was, for county politicos, a call to arms. A bitter legislative fight in the 1935 session was the result. Although Governor Merriam's administration naturally supported the idea advocated by the Club, the legislative moves were defeated in the State Senate. But it had a salubrious after-effect. The state's supervision of county roads thereafter became intense. Many of the basic reforms the Club had sought came about as a result.

Another legislative fight erupted that year. Many insurance firms saw the Club as natural competition, with its services for members. They opposed what they considered advertising in the road signs, which bore the full names of the Club or its counterpart in the northern part of the state. The Craig Bill to outlaw the signs was tossed into the hopper; it would have seriously hurt the uniformity of signs throughout the state. The Club reacted with alacrity.

From 1923 to 1933, the Club had paid from 99.79 percent to 60 percent of the costs of all such sign work in its southern California area. A compromise of sorts was finally reached that pacified the insurance firms. Both clubs agreed to use an inconspicuous insignia on the signs rather than their full names. Still, it was but a delaying action. Constant accusations were falsely made that the clubs profited from sign-posting. Too, many local officials were anxious to take over with sign work to increase their staffs, even though the State Highway Department defended the clubs. The argument was to continue.

Meanwhile, vaguely hopeful changes in the economic tide appeared. Directors were told that in the first eighty-six days of 1934 membership had dropped off only 1,571, compared with 7,343 members for the same period in 1933. It was a questionable victory to claim—but any victory was better than none.

Staffers speculated like everyone else. Had the country at last "turned the corner"? About the same time the employees' Ten-Year Club formally

PLATE 87 *One of the Club's rousing legislative fights of 1935—opposing the Craig Bill, favored by competing insurance firms, which would outlaw the use of the Auto Club name on road signs posted by the Club. Even after a decision was made, the argument raged.*

expressed appreciation to the directors for serving without compensation over the past four difficult years and fighting to keep nearly 1,000 men and women employed.

By fall it truly appeared that the dire days were ending. Membership for the first nine months was down only 1,580 as compared to a net loss of 16,374 for the first nine months of 1933. But the Club intended to remedy even that drop. In a drive for new members, a temporary reduc-

156

tion in enrollment fee from $5 to $3 was initiated (of which $1.00 was for WESTWAYS). In addition, a campaign of visits by management to the district offices to encourage personnel was begun. Employees were asked to submit names of prospective members. Some 700 membership posters were spotted in official garages and other likely places. A new windshield sticker and sales pamphlet were also a part of the drive to find new members.

Legislative concerns remained prominent. The Club opposed a proposal by police officials for legislation to require fingerprints and photographs on

PLATE 88 *The "Life Is Just a Bowl of Cherries" philosophy of the early thirties was only a façade. The true grimness of those years was reflected in new cars—square, solemn, and subdued. But that was only a concern of the few Americans who could afford them.*

an operator's license. (Today the fingerprints are optional.) Also, it fought against legislation proposed by a group of hospitals and doctors calling for part of the gas tax to be used to pay the doctors and hospitals giving emergency aid and treatment when the injured motorist could not pay himself. It could be, as the Club saw it, a beginning wedge to raid the gas tax for other non-highway purposes.

The inflammable issue of the state's centralized control of all county roads led to a meeting of representatives of the California State Automobile Association and the Club. The northern club did not agree with the Club's plan as written. Its objections included a fear that an enlarged state department could be a political evil and would lead to a losing battle with county supervisors. Furthermore, the northern group claimed, it didn't seem a sound fiscal measure and would not avoid a local road tax. Rather than the Club's plan, the northern club suggested that highway funds going to county supervisors should be spent with state supervision and under a plan submitted to, and approved by, the State Department of Public Works. Other changes proposed included: an increase in the allotment of money to cities by one-fourth cent, to be expended under state supervision; calling the state highway commission to give full time in return for appropriate salaries. After discussion, it was decided by Club officials that the northern suggestion would only entrench county supervisors more, but that it would be better than nothing if the Club's plan failed to survive the fight in the legislature.

From 1930 to 1935, the American had scrambled as never before in search of a dollar. Recovery had been slow. Yet by the beginning of mid-decade, it seemed that the worst had come and gone. It could hardly be said that business was booming. But, compared to the rock bottom of a few years before, businessmen could again face the future with some hope. The Club had made it through. A bit beaten and battered, for sure! But ready to build once again.

Chapter 11

GIVE IT THE GAS

If you don't give me an order, I'll vote for Him again!

—Salesman's calling card, 1935

AMERICA never "turned the corner." It edged around it, inch by tedious inch. In 1935 "recovery" was still lagging. President Roosevelt was under attack from all directions, and his confident predictions and revolutionary moves were challenged. The NRA seemed to be creating more controversy than production. The Agricultural Adjustment Administration was being questioned. No one really knew if it had aided farmers. Huey Long was in full glory. Dr. Townsend had his own curious army.

The great dust storms still raged and unhappy migrants roamed, the ancient jalopies hung together with spit and wire. But all Americans had become more nomadic. There were some three million more cars on the roads in 1937 than in 1929. More new cars weren't necessarily being bought, but old cars were kept going. And families who had never strayed more than a hundred miles from home were now wandering by auto, seeking jobs or visiting kin who had settled elsewhere.

A new misadventure had hit the auto industry—"streamlining." The auto of 1934 and 1935 was a bulbous monstrosity, due to the overworked eagerness of designers to keep pace with furniture and household gadgets. Obesity, not straight, simple lines, was the fad of the time, and even urban buses were flamboyantly designed to withstand the "airflow" when edging down Main Street at fifteen miles an hour. Freeways, expressways or whatever their name might be, were emerging, and motorists realized for the first time the glory of bypassing towns and clutter on a fast trip.

A new wonder was being born that was to soon become a fixture of American life. In 1929 a bacteriologist, Arthur B. Sherwood, had built a tiny cabin on wheels for his family. He built a few more, showed one at the Detroit Automobile Show of 1930 and—presto!— was soon manufacturing trailers. By 1936, it was estimated some 160,-000 trailers were roaming the byways of America.

In far-off Europe the sounds of war became increasingly ominous as the last half of the thirties loomed ahead. But that was *their* worry.

A climate of cautious optimism had begun to emerge at the Club by the beginning of 1935.

Recovery *was* a reality, staffers decided, although the bustling, carefree twenties were long ago and far away. The Club, unlike thousands of other enterprises, had weathered the storm. The years of declining membership and insurance were past. It had, of course, called for drastic measures. In 1934 the total operating cost was nearly $600,000 less than 1930, a decrease of 34 percent. During the same period, membership had declined 39 percent. But the Club had come through. It was operating under a balanced budget, and there was nearly $5 million in sound securities with the Exchange as a reserve.

In February, Harry Bauer was reelected president for the sixth time (and was to continue on until 1959). A clue to the Club's survival during the grim Depression can be traced to this outstanding leader, as well as to the actions of the other directors. Bauer was deeply involved in a variety of enterprises over these years. He was president of the Southern California Edison Company, as well as a director of the California Bank, the Title Insurance and Trust Company, the Spring Street Realty Company and a trustee of both University of Southern California and California Institute of Technology. He was typical of the leadership during those trying years.

All directors were important business or civic leaders. For example, directors during that decade included Allen C. Balch, a public utility executive; Harry Chandler, publisher of the Los Angeles *Times;* financier Henry W. Keller; Alexander Macbeth, president of the Southern Counties Gas Co.; attorney Henry S. McKay; Horace G. Miller, president of United Iron Works; Stuart O'Melveny, president of Title Insurance and Trust Co.; Joesph F. Sartori, president of the Security First National Bank; and George M. Wallace, also a president of the bank.

W. L. Valentine, Bauer's predecessor as president (1921–26), was of similar background. He was president of both Fullerton Oil Co. and Robinson's department store during his career, as well as a director of the Security First National Bank. Backing up these unpaid directors was Standish L. Mitchell, secretary and general manager, who was to serve until 1957 and be the recognized dean of motor club general managers in the West.

During the last half of the thirties, the Club was to surge back and surpass its old position under such leadership. At the beginning of 1934, membership was at a low of 81,560. In the five years to follow, it climbed steadily, until by 1939, it was up to 121,808. It still had not reached the old high of the pre-Depression days, but the growth was healthy.

The insurance Exchange also showed a similar steady increase. In 1934 there were 53,544 policies issued. Each year the business continued to swell, until by 1939, there were 94,004 policies with over $3 million in exchange premiums coming in. The Finance Department, too, showed steady growth. Out of 14,381 contracts issued for financing autos between 1930 and 1935, there had been only sixteen repossessions out of total loans amounting to $8,453,512. As the department grew, it was able to reduce rates to 4½ percent, extend contracts to twenty-four months and ask for one-third to 40 percent in down payments.

By December, 1935, directors were able to restore salaries of staffers which had been reduced 7½ percent in 1932 and also reestablish Christmas bonuses which had been eliminated in 1930.

With the reversal in fortune came new services. Two added aids to members included a new service to help those who'd misplaced or lost their keys, and a bail bond service to save time and money for those members unfortunate enough to tangle with John Law. A free Outing Show was added to annual Club events and was soon drawing 200,000 people a year.

The Club was now deeply immersed in the seemingly eternal drive to bring a rich harvest of tourist dollars to southern California. Along with such groups as the All Year Club, it rendered a variety of free services to keep the immigrant dollar, which averaged some $215 million each year during the thirties, pouring into the area.

The vast complexities of helping both members and nonmembers burgeoned with each year. The annual report of 1938 gives some clue to the activities. Staffers were involved with such diverse chores as aiding members in traffic court, handling 91,716 calls for emergency road service (with the patrols covering 302,213 miles that year), handling travel arrangements for members and issuing some 171,583 licenses. The list went on and on: there were 114 new Club maps issued that year; reservations were made in 18,150 hotels. The Public Safety Bureau appealed to nearly 300,000 people with safety films, while the Outing Bureau handled 20,835 calls. A total of more than 40,000 temporary and permanent

PLATE *89* *Between 1934 and 1941, popular Outing Shows were held in the patio of the Auto Club headquarters. Here a large crowd gathers to watch Chief of Police Davis' crack pistol team perform in early 1934.*

signs were erected, and the Speakers' Bureau filled 1,052 engagements. The Theft Department recovered 563 autos and the Touring Bureau aided more than a million and a half people with travel questions.

It was also a vigorous half decade in the perennial hassle over legislative matters in Sacramento. Highway problems involving the expenditures of funds, with the old bugaboo of north-south allocation of tax dollars, did not disappear. The Club protested to Governor Merriam and highway officials about what they felt was illegal discrimination and, in January, 1937, asked that the proposed current budget for state highways be revised. More attention should be given to the volume of traffic accidents in spending highway money, the Club felt. The appeal was successful, and one result was an increase in state highway funds for the Arroyo Seco Parkway, later to become the Pasadena Freeway.

The continuing wrangle between "cow country" legislators, eager to build often too lavish farm-to-market roads in their areas, and the urbanites, who needed funds to meet the population growth with its resultant wear and tear, did not abate. The Club opposed new state highways, fighting instead to improve and build the existing state routes. The Club also opposed any increase in the state gasoline tax, defending the California motorist's position of being subject to less total tax than in the majority of states. (California was paid a 3-cent-per-gallon fuel tax while the average for other states in the U.S. was 4½ cents per gallon.)

The legislature in 1935 was to add an innovation to taxation on motorists. It was the Vehicle License Fee Act, or "in lieu tax on motor vehicles," which was a substitute for the previous local personal property tax. The funds raised were used in part to pay the remaining principal and interest on outstanding state highway bonds; the balance was returned, one half to the counties and the other half to the cities.

Even at this time, the Club saw looming the crisis in urban travel. In 1937 the directors instructed the Club's engineers to study the problem and suggest long-range plans. In January, 1938, the engineers informed directors of their conclusion: a system of freeways in the Los Angeles metropolitan area. The next year the Club supported legislation defining freeways and authorizing initial construction.

During the 1939 session, the Club was to secure the enactment of Assembly Bill 693, an enabling act to permit the organizing of metropolitan transportation districts, which would prepare motorway plans and other facilities and come up with financing ideas. (The Club was unsuccessful, however, in persuading the cities in Los Angeles County to establish such a district.)

The thirties brought, in spite of the Depression, a constantly increasing revenue for state and county highway expansion and improvement, thanks to a growing auomotive registration, which meant added gas tax revenue. The additional one-cent gas tax revenue from 1927 helped, of course. The Club had pushed for the original two-cents-per-gallon tax in 1923 and the one-cent increase in 1927. (Compared to the 1963 legislation which increased the state gas tax to seven cents per gallon, the earlier bills were indeed modest.)

These early gas taxes met the state's needs, as a glance at a highway revenue and balance sheet for 1936 indicates. The three-cent gas tax brought in $36 million, and registration and weight fees another $10 million. That year's totals were $46 million, excluding federal aid.

It was a flamboyant era for the highway department, and its staffers did remarkable work. The Ridge Route alternate was completed, as was the Santa Ana Canyon Road, the viaduct near Barstow, widening of the Roosevelt Highway north of Santa Monica, construction of Sepulveda Blvd. from Ventura Blvd. to Sunset, and reconstruction of the historic San Marcos Pass in Santa Barbara County.

A variety of lesser projects were also finished. The period between 1935 and 1939 saw elimination of curves in the Cuesta Grade, relocation of the Grapevine Canyon Highway, the Figueroa Street aqueduct and tunnels, a separated highway in Montecito, and completion of part of the Pasadena Freeway which was not to be dedicated until December 30, 1940.

In 1936 San Francisco celebrated a great event: the dedication of the Bay Bridge. Governor Merriam sounded the tenor of the legislative act when, at the November 12 opening ceremony, he proclaimed: "This bridge belongs to this generation. We built it and we shall pay for it. . . . When the youths of today become the citizens of tomorrow, they will use it without cost."

But the good governor failed to reckon with the devious ways of politics. Although the act provided that the bridge would be free without toll when the indebtedness was paid, the 1959 legislature was persuaded otherwise. Today, toll is still paid to finance a rapid transit tube for passenger rail transits exclusively from San Francisco to Oakland. The "youth" of yester-year pays on. In 1937 the Golden Gate Bridge, built by a special district with state highway funds paying for the approaches, was opened for traffic.

The desperate search for the tax dollar led politicians into every possible crevice and cranny. During the thirties the state general fund was heavy with red ink, and the administration eagerly tried again and again to raid the highway revenues to make up the difference. Directors knew that if ever the gas tax were diverted to meet other needs, it would undoubtedly become a fixture as a handy source of funds, and the motorist would suffer. For this reason, the Club and its northern counterpart both refused to go along with some motor organizations calling for a gas tax increase.

The state tax system was finally revised to meet general fund needs; otherwise the treasury would have faced bankruptcy. But politicians eager to get highway funds diverted to their own causes persisted. Many such

166

proposals were made in legislative sessions between 1931 and 1937. A few were mildly successful, and during the 1933 and 1935 sessions the Club really had to fight hard to preserve highway funds for highway purposes. But, in the end, it won the day.

Yet, it was clear there was only one permanent solution. The Club knew a constitutional amendment, presented to the people, was necessary to avoid the constant threats of raids during each legislative session.

In 1936 a variety of forces joined in this effort, circulating initiative petitions to stop diversion. It was to be voted on in November. The Club allied itself with such groups as the Redwood Empire Association, the Associated General Contractors, the western representative of the National Highway Users Conference, the California Federation of Labor, the League of California Municipalities and many boards of supervisors and chambers of commerce. The California State Automobile Association in the north opposed the petition, known as No. 10, claiming it had technical defects. It was a bitter battle, with the Club's position winning in southern California, but losing in the north. The measure was defeated.

Now a new drive to save highway funds for highways had to be mounted. After seemingly endless conferences, a new anti-diversion constitutional amendment was prepared, known as SCA 28, and presented to the legislature. It was authored by William Knowland, then in the state Senate. A tough legislative fight followed, but SCA 28 finally gained legislative approval and was assured a place on the November, 1938, ballot. Before the general election, there was a vigorous educational campaign with the voting public. The amendment won 1,505,043 to 766,063.

The issue has not ended yet. Efforts have continued against the amendment by parties interested in using the gas tax for other purposes. Yet, if the Club and its allies had not fought the long fight, today's elaborate highway system would most assuredly have been seriously delayed. Probably the "pay-as-you-go" system still in effect would have been disrupted again and again by fund diversions, and the only recourse would have been massive bond issues that would, no doubt, have doubled the total cost of today's highways and freeways.

With the gradual onset of better times, the Club again was aggressively busy. Typical was a decision of the Finance Department. By January, 1935, automobile sales were again on the climb. Business had doubled in one month and was well over the same month a year before. Directors authorized some eighteen-month contracts with a 40 percent down payment and others with half down in a move to give better service and increase both insurance and membership.

Hopes for the International Pacific Highway were reborn. A newspaper publisher from Panama visited California with a finance plan calling for an international corporation controlled by the seven Central and South American countries interested in the project.

By March, 1935, President Bauer was able to announce a positive trend: "For almost four years your club successfully met the conditions occasioned by consistent decrease in the number of members. The turn came last June (1934) and since that time there has been a steady and consistent gain in the number of members." That month there was a net gain of 690 members, the tenth consecutive month of growth, which had added up to a total gain of 2,277. Things were, indeed, moving again. The All Year Club reported a lively increase in tourists about the same time, and a survey showed 96 percent apartment house occupancy.

With the quickening of business activity came attendant problems. Los Angeles voters were asked to consider a local measure to authorize jitney buses. Directors, remembering the chaos of seventeen years before when junky used autos, serving as buses, congested the downtown area, called for the Club to oppose the measure. Also at this time the Arizona Auto Club was having more troubles. The reason: it was serving more tourists than its own members. It called on the Club for aid, since most of these same tourists were bound for southern California.

The competition for the auto owners' interest dollar was in full swing by now. The Finance Department studied rates charged by Bank of America and General Motors Acceptance Corporation and concluded the Club should compete by reducing its rates from 6 to 4½ percent and, at the same time, reduce the amount of earnings returned to reserve from 1 percent to half of 1 percent. The Security and California banks were also persuaded to reduce their charge on loans to the Finance Department from 4 to 3 percent. With the change, the department could still compete and show a profit, which was enough to cover the half of 1 percent for transfer to the reserves.

As the end of 1935 approached, membership stood at 90,084, a net gain of 10½ percent for the year, or 8,524 new members.

PLATE 90 *Developed from a "cabin on wheels," some 160,000 trailers were roaming America by 1936. Here, trailers, along with other camping equipment, attract many visitors to one of the Club's free Outing Shows.*

It continued to climb as spring came, and in the annual report, issued in March, 1936, President Bauer could happily title his remarks "Best Year in a Decade."

About that time J. Allen Davis prepared a remarkable summation for the sales force of the Club. It showed the outstanding record of Club achievement in legislative efforts that had aided the motorist. Not only could California boast of close to the lowest motor vehicle taxes, but Davis traced the many special proposals the Club helped defeat that would have increased such taxes or diverted motor vehicle revenue for other uses. The report also listed the constructive legislation for highways and vehicles that had been either initiated or supported by the Club. Yet, even while directors paused to revel briefly and with pardonable pride over the Davis report, new matters were brewing. One was a curious addition to our happy land, the parking meter. The Club didn't know exactly what stand to take on the proposal to put meters on downtown Los Angeles streets. A letter from the Oklahoma Auto Club—where city meters were first installed—indicated the pros and cons. It was decided more study was needed. A month later the matter was still being pondered cautiously. The AAA had come out against the urban money-makers, although many a city looked with relish on the new source of income.

The International Pacific Highway quandary continued. The planned route of the highway down the west coast had suddenly been abandoned by the Mexican government in favor of a route through Chihuahua and Durango. A few months later, information indicated that the Mexican government itself intended to completely abandon its interest in the highway, leaving it all up to the individual states of Mexico. The Club decided it best not to enter the controversy. The reason became clear after Mr. Henry W. Keller visited Mexico City. While opinion was divided on the matter, the Southern Pacific Railway of Mexico had been blocking highway construction. To add to the dilemma, the federal government of Mexico was broke. The oil companies of Mexico favored the highway but had few resources with which to help.

By the end of 1936, the Club was thriving once again, and the horrendous days of Depression seemed far away. Gross membership stood at 103,147. The long climb back had started.

Chapter 12

THE PREWAR BUSTLE

"The U.S.A. would be better off if that big, sprawling, incoherent, shape-less, slobbering, civic idiot in the family of American communities, the city of Los Angeles, could be declared incompetent and placed in charge of a guardian like any individual mental defective."

—Westbrook Pegler, 1937

By 1937 a growing national pastime reached full flower: deprecating Los Angeles. But the eastern pundits and columnists who could intimidate the politicians and celebrities of Washington and New York City with just a nasty adjective could never really fluster the Angeleno.

East Coast and San Francisco journalists ridiculed Los Angeles for its hot dog stands that looked like hot dogs, informal street wear, cultists and kooks, but their bitter jibes only caused chuckles (and often proud ones at that) in much maligned southern California. For the vast hordes of newcomers were seekers and experimenters, frequently crass but filled with an uncontrollable vigor, eagerness and a shocking unconcern for what was traditional and correct. Here on the soft frontier, U.S. industry and business found a great test tube in which to experiment with new ideas in design and merchandising. "Southern Californians are like anyone else—only more so," summed up one observer.

Two major issues dominated the national scene in 1937: labor on the march and President Roosevelt's knockdown fight with the Supreme Court. But even more important matters were to affect America. Franco was besieging Madrid with the aid of Mussolini, and Japan was attacking China.

Lesser events intrigued the average citizen, however. The royal romance between Wally and the Duke of Windsor was still the subject of endless discussion, as was the Joe Louis-Jim Braddock fight at Chicago. Californians worried as more Dust Bowlers, ruined by the drought, arrived. Amelia Earhart's disappearance became a national mystery. "The Big Apple" swept the land as the latest dance craze.

In August came the recession of 1937, a frightening condition for already wary Americans. It was to slowly fade away as an apprehensive public watched. But, by the next summer, there were more serious concerns. In September, Neville Chamberlain returned from meeting Hitler to announce: "I believe it is peace in our time. . . ." But some still heard the thunder of the marching boots.

Distractions and escapes caught the public fancy. Louis knocked out Schmeling. Howard Hughes flew around the world, and the unknown aviator Corrigan mistakenly flew to Ireland after filing flight plans for

California. "Monopoly," which gave every man a chance to play million-aire, was still the fad game, and "A Tisket, a Tasket" was a hit tune. The business index began to climb, and, despite massive unemployment, hope shone amidst the black clouds of threatened war.

With Hitler's increasing demands, America became enmeshed in the business of supplying for war by a complicated series of moves—diplo-matic and otherwise. Roosevelt steadily pressed for increasing interven-tion. America, unsure and puzzled, waited. Orson Welles panicked the U.S. with a too realistic radio show, based on H. G. Wells's *War of the Worlds,* which dramatized a Martian invasion.

New developments moved war closer in the months to come. Germany and Russia signed a nonaggression pact.

The auto of 1937 had come a long way since that distant night of December 13, 1900, when the ten Club founders met to form what was to become, sixty-eight years later, an organization of 850,000 members. No one can accurately say precisely when the auto ceased to be a toy and became a necessity. Some authorities say 1910 was the turning point. The Spindletop gusher was no doubt a factor, as was the first Autocar driven with a shaft rather than being chain-driven. Locomobile, with a gas-driven, four-cylinder, water-cooled, front-mounted engine, gave know-ing men pause at that crucial time. Still, the attrition rate was startling when one looks back. Out of some 300 companies making autos in 1910, only four—Cadillac, Buick, Ford and Oldsmobile—survive today.

The evolution toward a great industry had been slow—the self-starter, the all-steel body and, finally, the listing of motor companies on the New York Stock Exchange. In the twenties, standardization came along with selective gear transmissions and block-cast cylinders. There had been shortages during World War I, followed by an auto production boom with some 150 new companies rushing into business in the first five postwar years. Between the war and the Depression, customers turned more and more to low-priced cars. The Crash was to wipe out these same, new, low-priced producers. But by 1930 most Americans ac-cepted the auto as a basic necessity of life; there were some 23 million passenger cars and 3.55 million trucks and buses on U.S. roads.

Meanwhile, several firms had moved upward as solid trade names known to every American. Buick, started in 1903 by David Buick, a plumbing-ware supplier, was in its heyday by the thirties. It came out

PLATE *91 There were some 300 automobile manufacturers in the United States in 1910, and many of their models that are no longer in existence—like the once-popular Packard—were still being produced in the late 1930s.*

with a vacuum-operated clutch in 1932, rear coil springs in 1938, and was to present two dual downdraft carburetors in 1940.

Cadillac came into being as an engine-building company, formally founded in 1903 by Henry M. Leland, a man with a fetish for precision. He was to lead the way to fine tolerances in auto manufacture. His first autos, priced at $750, were to grow in reputation in the decades to follow. In 1930, Cadillac went after the affluent buyer with its new V-16, some models costing over $8,000.

The first Chevrolet was manufactured in 1911. Its founder, the master automaker William C. Durant, worked with the Swiss race driver Louis Chevrolet to steadily develop and refine the low-priced roadsters and touring cars, and by the mid-twenties, it was the most popular low-priced car in the U.S. In 1929, Chevrolet was to switch from its four-cylinder design to six cylinders.

While few radical changes of design were made, Chevrolet went along in 1935 with other General Motors cars—which it had become part of in 1918—with a "Turret Top" all-steel body. Chevy was to become, most authorities agree, the most important division in the massive General Motors array of names.

Walter Chrysler, a trained executive with Buick and Willys-Overland, was not to emerge until 1925 with the Maxwell Motor Company as the nucleus for his auto empire. In the years to come, Chrysler, a perfectionist in engineering, was to hire premier designers in his fight to gain a strong share of the market for "America's most powerful motor car," as it was advertised.

On its tenth anniversary, Chrysler introduced the Airflow series—a radical departure in design. The cars had 55 percent of their weight supported on the front wheels and only 45 percent on the rear, with leaf springs to give them the "floating" quality that the advertising heralded. In an era of concern over air friction, the Chrysler was designed to reduce wind resistance with a tapering body, rounded and sloping front and no real fenders. It was, alas, a commercial flop, but it did provide design ideas that would be adapted.

John and Horace Dodge had their own dependable product by 1914—a vehicle that John J. "Black Jack" Pershing used as his personal auto in his campaign against Pancho Villa. And it was also the official American Expeditionary Force car in World War I. In 1928, Dodge was purchased by Chrysler.

The Franklin was still seen on Los Angeles streets in the 1930s (the firm produced autos until 1934), while Hudson continued from 1909 until 1954 when it was absorbed by American Motors. One of the most famous of these Hudson styles was the Terraplane, an inexpensive car that was produced between 1933 and 1942.

The first Lincoln rolled off the assembly line in 1921; the popular Lincoln Zephyr, with a streamlined, frameless body and twelve-cylinder engine, came in 1935 and set the trend at Ford—and later the entire industry—for having an auto styling department, rather than a single artist. The famed Lincoln Continental was introduced in 1939. It was patterned after European design and—like the popular Cord—had a box-like body, which later became a classic.

PLATES *92 and 93   Only four of the 1910 car companies survive today—Cadillac, Buick, Ford and Oldsmobile. And the Hupmobile, the Willys, the Franklin and the Chandler, all on the road in the 1930s, are now curiosities.*

Other makes, now gone, were still around in 1937. Nash was to join with Hudson and become American Motors in 1954. Oakland was to be the ancestor of today's Pontiac, while the once important Packard name was to fade away soon after the mid-fifties merger with Studebaker.

The pioneer Studebaker, first a buggy back in 1857, was to continue until recently, while the Overland, Chandler, Autocar and scores of others chugged off over the horizon of auto history. The Oldsmobile, the oldest American car still being produced (preceding the Ford by six years), became part of General Motors in 1908 and, one could assume, was the auto that General Motors used to test new ideas over the years. All of these names and models roamed the roads and highways of southern California in the mid-thirties.

While new problems emerged for the Automobile Club, old ones persisted for the directors and staff during those years.

The battle went on between north and south over the allocation of highway funds, with the Club protesting repeatedly to Governor Merriam. One Club suggestion was that greater thought be given to the traffic volume and highway accidents in planning the highway budget. As a result, the state allowed more funds for the Arroyo Seco Parkway (now the Pasadena Freeway) and work on Figueroa Street and Olympic Boulevard.

Membership at the beginning of 1937 was 103,147, and it continued to climb at a slow, but steady, rate in the next three years.

A prime concern during this eventful period was the International Pacific Highway. A convention was held at Mazatlán in February of 1937. President Herrera of Mexico was present to endorse the project and promise support. Mexico's federal government agreed to build the highway from Tepic to Guadalajara, the most difficult part of the construction, and the Mexican states were to finance their share. (The Club itself spent only $150 a month for one contact man in this effort.)

Meanwhile, the Banks of London and Mexico issued bonds that had been guaranteed by the Mexican government by the impounding of gas tax revenue. The financing of the section down the west coast of Mexico from Nogales to Mexico City was also assured by December, 1937. By October, 1938, General Cardenas had promised 100,000 more pesos (about $20,500) to the project. Additional pesos came from the various Mexican states involved. Slowly, the route plans developed.

The Club's sound management and caution during the desperate early years of the Depression had resulted in an accumulation of savings, which an exchange report on investment securities illustrated clearly. The market value stood at $5,394,732.21 as compared with the securities' book value of $4,748,207.38, an increase of $646,524.83. The original cost, excluding accrued interest, was $4,848,385.85.

Generally speaking, between 1937 and 1940, the north continued to be shown what the Club felt was favoritism on the matter of highway funds. Bills before the legislature told the story. Typical was one in the spring of 1937 that called for additions to the state highway system, giving 767.1 miles of new road in the north and only 358.1 miles to the south. The Club was able to defeat this bill. Too, the director of the Department of Motor Vehicles was involved in a series of bills that had antagonized finance companies and auto dealers.

As always, there were forces out to raid the gas tax revenue, and Los Angeles County was reportedly attempting to use some $2 million in gas tax funds to repay a loan for unemployment relief, a move the Club protested. The Club also opposed the Pacific Electric Railway Company when it applied for a franchise to operate a bus service on the Arroyo Seco Parkway.

At times the Club joined forces with the northern club. One such alliance was a plan for an initiative constitutional amendment to reorganize the State Highway Commission so that the five members would serve staggered terms and have full control over both highways and the California Highway Patrol. The objective was to provide unified control and remove the commission from the political control of the governor as much as possible, avoiding, by this means, highway construction for purely political reasons.

In 1938 two propositions found their way onto the ballot, one known as the anti-diversion gasoline tax measure to eliminate such problems as Los Angeles County's recent bid to acquire gas funds for unemployment relief, and the other to reorganize the Highway Commission. The November vote saw the anti-diversion amendment adopted by a substantial margin, but the Commission change defeated. It had been an expensive fight for the Club: costs for advertising and other campaign measures were $127,-001.52.

Such legislative battles seemed never-ending. By January, 1939, the

Club was again active, opposing moves for substantial additions to the state highway system and an increase in the gas tax. It also endorsed a proposal by the League of Municipalities to require counties to set up a budget for road and street expenditures, with the approval of the State Highway Commission and the Department of Public Works; so, too, did it support a bill placing city streets on an equal footing with rural roads in such expenditures. An assembly bill approved by the Club was drafted and introduced in 1939 to permit local authorities to create districts for studying and planning various transportation systems.

Four thousand bills were introduced during the lively 1939 Sacramento session, 186 affecting the operation of motor vehicles and 120 related to streets and highways. As always, the yearly dispute over increasing the gas tax warmed. The Club, pointing out that gas was more heavily taxed than any other necessity (the price was then eighteen cents a gallon, including a 28 percent tax), fought political moves to increase the tax. The average state tax was then four and one-half cents per gallon; in California it was three cents. This, the Club explained, saved the California motorist some $26 million a year.

By 1939 the Club, along with other established organizations, faced one of the most devastating financial proposals the state had even seen. Known as "Ham 'n' Eggs," or "Thirty Dollars Every Thursday," it called for a massive increase in taxes to give certain oldsters $30 a week, which—as the proponents' theory went—would be spent to create limitless prosperity and an economic boom in the state. That it also threatened bankruptcy and chaos for the state didn't concern its backers.

The Club went to work with mailing pieces and press stories to defeat the initiative measure, spending some $5,000 in the process. The wild scheme was defeated at the polls.

Some issues of the time sound like an echo down the corridor of recent history. There was the crisis of street parking. Downtown merchants opposed the suggestion of curtailing it. Meanwhile, the idea of an elevated railway system—similar to a monorail in Germany—was being discussed.

Club staffers at this time were not only invited to board meetings to present facts and figures but encouraged to speak up whenever they disagreed. President Harry Bauer officially explained: ". . . if any member of the staff present at the meetings held opinions contrary to statements made or decisions reached, it was his obligation to state his views; that failing to do so would constitute approval of statements made and actions taken."

The routine functions of the various departments continued to grow in volume as the Depression days faded away. In 1937 a report showed that 17,283 permanent signs and more than 30,000 temporary ones went up. The Emergency Patrol, helping all motorists, gave emergency first aid and help to 52,148 people. Its familiar three-wheel vehicles covered 256,829 miles of California roads. More than 573,000 people called the Touring Bureau, which gave out over 6 million maps and replied to 40,000 inquiries.

By the end of that year, membership stood at 114,001. The directors then were Bauer, Harry Chandler, Henry W. Keller, Horace G. Miller, W. L. Valentine, George M. Wallace, A. C. Balch, Alexander B. Macbeth and Henry S. MacKay.

The thorny issue of freeways—or motorways, as they were called at the time—was actively debated even thirty years ago. The 1937 Metropolitan Traffic Survey was sent to more than a thousand interested outlets in the state, while newspapers like the *Christian Science Monitor*, New York *Times* and Chicago *Tribune* gave it national attention. Many downtown businessmen were lukewarm to the Survey's suggestion that freeways were the hope of the future. Many held that what was good enough for their fathers or customers—namely streetcars—was good enough for the Los Angeles public. But the Club thought otherwise, since the study showed 80 percent of the public wanted to drive and that only 20 percent preferred streetcars. The majority must be provided with freeways, the report concluded. Freeways would save motorists a cent a mile, the Club estimated, because it would no longer be necessary to stop and shift at surface cross streets or for pedestrians.

Another happy project was born in January, 1939, in WESTWAYS. Phil Townsend Hanna had been tracing and collecting the origins of California place names for some ten years. In the first issue that year the first group was published. Others followed, and were later published in book form. It was a definitive piece of Californiana and a valuable reference work.

A financial study also was made that year. It showed that in 1938 alone the Club had saved members $305,000 in 91,716 calls for emergency road service when Club costs were compared with commercial rates. Furthermore, the Adjustment and Traffic Department, busy at collecting and adjusting bail bonds, had saved members $300,000. By then there were 400 stations with 1,900 trained employees to give emergency road service; insurance protection saved more than $16 million for subscribers.

The three years were marked by steady and happy growth. Membership had continued to climb. The Exchange had grown. It seemed that all was well again by late summer of 1939.

But forces far away were to change the entire world, and the Club was not immune.

September 1, 1939, started much like any other day in Los Angeles. Stores were bustling with activity as parents bought clothes for the coming school year, and fans argued over the coming fate of USC and UCLA in football.

In distant Berlin that day, in the hot and humid Kroll Opera House, Adolf Hitler, wearing a field-gray tunic and black trousers, stood on the rostrum. Faces of uniformed listeners glistened with sweat as they looked up at Der Führer under the Nazi silver eagle. It was the night before German patrols entered Poland.

"Since 5:45 o'clock this morning enemy fire has been returned," he announced. Two days later England and France declared war.

World War II had come.

Chapter 13

A CALM BEFORE THE STORM

*"Business activity in California showed a marked advance in November–
December, 1939, spurred by the European war and the repudiation of the
Ham 'n' Eggs pension plan at the polls . . ."*

—Encyclopaedia Britannica
Yearbook 1940.

I T WAS A time of pause by 1939, of a curious calm between the horror of the Depression just passed and the impending chaos of war ahead. Yet those days, as they say in southern California, had the smell of "earthquake weather." People preferred to look the other way, to believe what seemed certain was—just perhaps—not so. Selective service wouldn't last—really. Hitler couldn't hold out—really. Something good would happen soon—really.

Meanwhile, business volume grew steadily. There were new dances, new tunes and football games to worry about. Everyone was eager to lose himself in such escapes.

By the late thirties and early forties an auto cult emerged, made up of those who looked back and savored the vehicles of the past. The Cord L and Cord L 180, which had come in 1929 and 1935 respectively and created major excitement, were typical. These designs, both offsprings of the Auburn, were to survive as dream cars of aficionados. The 810 with concealed door hinges and "coffin nose," as streetcorner chortlers dubbed it, also boasted disappearing headlights, no running boards and louvers to replace the conventional radiator.

Also, older and more hallowed autos were no longer considered worn-out and worthless, but became prized possessions. The first stock Dusenberg had emerged in 1920 with hydraulic, four-wheel brakes. The limousine reputedly could do 130 mph in a race. By the time of the first supercharger, the Model SJ of 1932, the Dusenberg had become synonymous with utter prestige and affluence. So, too, was the Marmon which had a brief history as a glamour car—until the firm disappeared into receivership in 1927. For many years, from 1906 to 1931, the Kissel had lingered on the American scene as every young man's dream. The "Gold Bug," a sports model, like the Mercer Racebout (1910–15), was, indeed, the forerunner of today's sports cars.

Not to be neglected among such glamour cars was the famed Pierce-Arrow, which officially appeared in 1909. It cost between $5,000 and $9,000 and was made with infinitely refined detail. The name was to linger where great autos were discussed even after Studebaker absorbed the firm.

A legend soon after its time was the famed Stutz Bearcat, which had remained popular until the early 1930s but disappeared in 1935.

All of the glamour cars, including the less sparkling Rickenbacker sports sedan, the Moon Continental Six, the DuPont LeMans speedster and the Jordan Speedboy, were to fade slowly from the highways of America. Yet, as fast as these glamour cars left the highways, fanciers of old autos searched junk piles and garages for the abandoned beauties to give them new life.

Meanwhile, at the Club, the seasoned veterans who had weathered the Depression's grim days watched with calm delight as the membership continued to grow and the southern California economy showed new vigor.

Scores of auto clubs had flourished and died in this period, like hundreds of auto trade names which had come and gone. But the Automobile Club of Southern California had survived and prospered.

The officers of the Club were old allies by 1940: President Harry Bauer; Alexander Macbeth, first vice president; Henry Keller, second vice president; Standish Mitchell, secretary and general manager; Ralph Reynolds, assistant secretary. All had been elected in 1935. Most of the directors were, similarly, old-timers in facing the often complicated problems facing the Club.

The directors maintained their intense and enthusiastic interest in the building of the International Pacific Highway. On April 4, 1940, Glenn Duckworth of the Club Touring Bureau reported to them on the highway's barranca section which he had covered in a Club car. He'd made the trip without difficulty, he said. Mr. Keller reported regularly on contract development on the section between Nogales and Mexico City. Congress had appropriated $20 million for the highway from Mexico City to Panama. But later a question arose whether the funds should be used for this proposed project or less important international highways. The political confusion soon became a moot point. The Mexico City–Panama highway was supposed to be completed by 1943 or 1944, but the North African invasion changed all this. Army engineers lost interest in a Panama highway and left its completion to the Bureau of Public Roads.

In 1940 the Arroyo Seco Parkway (Pasadena Freeway) had been completed by the State Highway Department, as had the Kings River Highway which had been started ten years before. Also, the first units of the divided highway through Cahuenga Pass was under way. Ahead were trying days for such projects, however. Road and highway construction was to be greatly curtailed due to lack of men, material and funds, even though the Club was to urge the federal government to aid in building and maintaining strategic and defense highways in the state. These included such projects as 300 miles of defense access roads costing more than $28 million, as well as a 5,600-mile network of strategic roads at an estimated cost of $150 million.

Old problems went on as legislators tried again and again to increase the state gasoline tax and motor vehicle taxes. The Club found it necessary to oppose these increases and to oppose also additions to the state highway

PLATE *94 The very incomplete state of the Arroyo Seco Parkway, August, 1938. The coming war slowed all highway construction, but, by 1940, the parkway was completed. It was later to be renamed the Pasadena Freeway, the first segment in Los Angeles' massive network of freeways, and the first freeway in California.*

PLATE 95 *War had its effects on the Club's popular Outing Shows, too. From 1934 to 1941, thousands of people came each year to see the newest in cars, trailers, camping equipment and girls. Three million attended in 1940. After the 1941 show, the military requested the event be stopped.*

system usually presented in the ratio of four miles in the north to one mile in the south. Nevertheless, the Club joined at times with the northern club, the California State Automobile Association, as an ally against mutually harmful bills. One measure would have repealed the presumption of innocence for those charged with a traffic violation. The bill also called for the redefinition of reckless driving to include any act of simple negligence. The Club opposed this move sponsored by certain peace officers. As one Club spokesman explained: "The police officials' attitude toward the motoring public in respect to speed traps, mail citations and plainclothesmen is much the same as that of the village constable of twenty-five years ago and goes back to the horse-and-buggy days of traffic enforcement methods."

Yet, despite these negative stands, the Club aided other measures. During those years they supported: a law to relieve nonresident motorists of obtaining nonresident permits, a bill to allow the Department of Public Works and local authorities to set speed zones in certain areas, and a measure to increase the speed limit on rural highways from 45 to 55 mph.

The Club worried about the municipal drive to place parking meters on downtown Los Angeles streets. To city fathers it was a tempting new source of income. The Club held that meters would indeed furnish revenue but cut down on badly needed road space for autos driving in the crowded area.

War ended the Outing Show, which had become a popular annual event sponsored by the Club. In April, 1940, more than 300,000 visitors attended the free show at Club headquarters which included such novelties as a "talking" Plymouth (long before the idea was to appear as a television series!), lumber-jack log-rolling, a High Sierra dog team and mountain pack team. The next year a half-million people came to see the last show before the military requested the event be stopped. (It was not revived after the war because the Club headquarers could not accommodate the huge crowds and elaborate exhibitions.)

The spring of 1939 brought what threatened to be a devastating financial crisis. Whether the Club was subject to income tax had been an old and complicated argument first joined in 1917. The Internal Revenue Department had given diverse rulings. In 1920 and 1924, it was held that the Club had to pay income tax; but, after many legal briefs and protests, the Commissioner of Internal Revenue ruled in 1927 that the Club was exempt as a non-profit service club with no part of its earnings being distributed to stockholders or members.

The Club admitted receiving insurance commissions placed for members in out-of-state companies, as well as certain rental payments and subscriptions to WESTWAYS. But it established that all of these revenues were used strictly for Club membership purposes and were not distributed as dividends or paid to members, directors or officers—except for those full-time officers on salary. Insurance commissions had been used to finance and pay off the mortgage of the headquarters building, and WESTWAYS income used to improve the magazine. A small percentage of the finance charges were used by the Finance Department as operating funds.

On March 17, 1939, the Club received a letter from the Commissioner of Internal Revenue. It advised that the previous ruling had been reversed. The Club was not only subject to paying federal income tax in the future, but the new ruling was retroactive to 1930. It was estimated the Club would have to pay delinquent taxes and penalties of over $350,000.

For two years Club attorneys conferred with officials of the IRD. By July, 1941, a compromise was reached. The Club accepted a taxable status beginning January, 1940, and the government waived payment on the prior taxes it had previously demanded.

By January, 1939, membership had climbed to 121,808. A lively debate at that time involved the proposed route for the Oxnard–San Juan Capistrano Highway and whether it should be routed through Santa Monica and the other beach cities. The Club opposed the beach route. At the same time the Club endorsed building the Hollywood Freeway as part of Route 101, even while directors disagreed with making it a toll highway. The obvious and simple reason was that many motorists wouldn't use it since the toll could be avoided by taking parallel routes.

The city was by now moving rapidly west and gaining more population density. The Club supported an idea to use Wilshire Boulevard as an artery for "off-center movement" traffic control during the morning and afternoon rush hours. The concept eliminated left turns at many intersections during rush hours, limited parking on Wilshire and coordinated the timing of signal lights.

The president's annual report for 1939 showed definite gains. The Insurance Exchange that year had offered members a new insurance feature—a "guest medical rider" which protected members against passenger injury. Bodily injury premium rates were reduced to save Club members over $800,000 in premiums for the year. The Finance Department also proudly announced a 41 percent increase in business for the year and introduced a twenty-four-month payment plan. Matters looked up in the north-south highway fight. Southern California had benefited in every county, the report showed, despite floods that year which had stopped construction in many places.

The Los Angeles parking meter conflict was in full fury by now. Mayor Bowron saw $500,000-a-year revenue for the city, but the city attorney ruled that while the city had a right to install the meters, it could not install them *just* to raise revenues. A lively city council session in the summer of 1940 found all the established powers of downtown Los Angeles opposing the meters and only the meter interests favoring them. Action was postponed by the council, and the matter was to simmer for years. It was apparent, however, that the downtown flood of motorists each day had to be offered some parking facilities. A study of off-street parking was initiated by the Club. Downtown businessmen feared that parking shortages would lose customers to suburban trade centers.

There was real cause for worry because as the city spread in all directions, suburbanites became more reluctant to make the trip into the traditional city center to shop. The great population boom brought on in part by servicemen who visited California during World War II (and later then returned to stay) had not yet come with its tract homes and new suburban commercial islands. But southern California was the land of oranges and sunshine to thousands of hopeful migrants even by then. Crossroad settlements turned into towns, and towns into cities. The Club's district offices sprouted up throughout southern California to meet the growing demand for its services.

At this time, district offices were located in: San Diego, Alhambra, Santa Maria, Taft, Ventura, Santa Monica, Pasadena, Porterville, Hollywood, San Bernardino, Long Beach, Glendale, Huntington Park, Highland Park, Pomona, Bellflower, San Fernando, Santa Paula, Burbank, Westwood, El Monte, Oceanside and East Los Angeles.

By January, 1941, the Club's future seemed assured and bright. The president's annual report that spring traced growth for the year and recalled the Club's forty-year history. Membership had increased 6,486 during the previous year to 128,394. There had been more than $6.5 million in insurance written, and the Finance Department could report that since July, 1930, it had financed many thousands of cars worth over $55 million. As for the state as a whole, the Club had forty-eight offices, while the California State Automobile Association in the north had thirty-five offices. Together they had 2,000 employees serving 231,000 members.

Within a few months the Club was to pass an even more important milestone. By August 31, 1941, total membership went to 137,779—the highest in Club history, surpassing by a few members the previous high point in 1930.

By then the realities of the war in Europe were evident nearly everywhere in the U.S. The British had faced Dunkirk in June, 1940, and France surrendered that same month. The great air battle of Britain had started. By September, 1940, the conscription act had been adopted. War production was in earnest. The U.S. had traded fifty destroyers to Great Britain and Roosevelt had defeated Willkie. In May, 1941, a state of unlimited national emergency had been proclaimed, and the next month the Nazis had invaded Russia. The U.S. was deeply involved in supplying besieged England by convoys of merchant ships. With all this, the Club naturally became increasingly involved in war-time activity.

The military asked for the cooperation of the Club in a variety of ways. For instance, the Club sign-posted military installations, provided touring information for relatives visiting military camps and aided in map making. It organized the Service Motor Corps with the northern club, enrolling volunteer motorists to pick up servicemen. The motorists were issued certificates of identification and the servicemen were to show passes and sign their names on a roll carried by the volunteer motorist.

California was still spinning its wheels in the quagmire of favoritism and political horse trading in highway matters. The persisting block of "cow county legislators"—usually from the northern part of the state— threatened to impede legislation unless they received a disproportionately large share of highway funds for their own areas. A report presented to the Club's board in 1941 spelled out what had happened over the years. Between 1912 and 1938, Los Angeles County motorists had contributed over $201 million to the state highway fund. Of this they had received back only $59 million in highway funds. The State Highway Commission continued to spend vast sums for "political roads" while it neglected such obvious problems as the increasing traffic load on the Bakersfield to Fresno route.

While southern California partisans muttered of state reapportionment and other means to overcome highway inequity, the war clouds darkened. Such parochial matters would soon take a back seat to the all-out fight for U.S. survival against the Axis threat—for, on December 7, 1941, the Japanese bombed Pearl Harbor.

Chapter 14

THE WAR YEARS

"We Americans have cleared our decks and taken our battle stations. We stand ready in the defense of our nation . . ."

—Franklin D. Roosevelt, Nov., 1941.

WHEN the Japanese bombed Pearl Harbor December 7, 1941, many Americans realized they had actually been at war for some time. U. S. Marines had been stationed in Iceland; industry was geared to "defense"; our ships had been sunk by the Nazis; everywhere men were in uniform; and Roosevelt's reelection over Willkie had been, in effect, a mandate for FDR to lead America toward commitment with England and away from isolationism.

New phrases had emerged: The Four Freedoms, Lend-Lease, War of Nerves. But old problems remained, despite the threat of war. Henry Ford had agreed for the first time to negotiate with a labor union, and in June, 1941, the CIO ended a four-and-a-half-year campaign with every major auto manufacturer in its camp. War in Europe had touched Detroit. Ford, Chrysler and General Motors announced they'd turn out aircraft sub-assemblies on their production lines which would be assembled elsewhere. By then a war-born, freakish newcomer in the automotive world had captured the attention of young America (even if you couldn't own one): the jeep. After eighteen months of testing at such chores as pulling field pieces, doing recon work, speeding over rutty roads at 60 mph, hauling weapons and men and functioning as a communication truck, it was officially decided the jeep was the greatest blessing to the soldier since draft beer. Said one Army authority: "Transportation in the U. S. Army is at least 50 percent superior to that of any other army in the world, and the Jeep can grab a great share of that glory."

It had been a bustling year, those nervous months before we entered the war. Life, as the old saw goes, had gone on—even skipping merrily along at times between the grim news of war. Shirley Temple, age twelve, came out of retirement to make four new movies, and Babe Ruth, caught up in patriotism, wandered into New York's defense bond headquarters to order $100,000 in bonds. *Pal Joey* was a Broadway hit along with *My Sister Eileen, Arsenic and Old Lace* and *Watch on the Rhine*. Hank Greenberg, baseball's highest-paid player ($55,000 a year), was inducted into the Army.

A harbinger of things to come was the sudden interest in the turbosupercharger that fateful year. Twenty-two years before, Dr. Sanford Moss had invented it. (The turbosupercharger compresses a plane's exhaust gases in the carburetor for increased energy when power is lost at high altitude due to less atmospheric oxygen.) Tried first in 1918, it had been forgotten until General Electric revived the Moss dream.

Autos played comic and tragic roles in the life of the land. One Boston citizen, following a pal's directions, was a bit bitter to find himself driving in a subway tunnel. Near Detroit another motorist went to sleep at the wheel and the famous Lone Ranger, idol of moppets, was dead. In Missouri a kindly passerby stopped to aid an injured motorist and stretched him out in a bed of poison ivy. And, in Washington, D.C., another motorist found a nude girl standing under a streetlight. She'd refused to give an engagement ring back to her boyfriend, and he'd taken all her clothes instead, she explained. The auto had, indeed, come a long way in less than fifty years.

By midsummer of 1941 deepening troubles had Price Administrator Leon Henderson in a turbojet-propelled tizzy of his own. Ford, Chrysler, Studebaker, Nash and Hudson had all announced price increases ranging from $10 to $53 an auto. Henderson, trying to hold the line, tangled with Chrysler when it refused to rescind the increase.

Meanwhile, oilmen were under stress as more and more aid was needed for Britain. Fifty U.S. oil tankers had been loaned to Britain. Harold Ickes, petroleum coordinator, asked that an additional 100 tankers be turned over to Britain—a step that would have sharply reduced our Atlantic fleet and made more critical the gas shortage on the East Coast.

Before Pearl Harbor, business and government teeter-tottered over national goals, but after war was declared the commitment to the long task ahead was solid. Every home and business felt the total impact overnight.

The Club was deeply involved by the Monday morning of December 8 with endless planning meetings and discussions. Problems came soon enough: dimouts, blackouts, tire and gas rationing, map-making activities for defense authorities, sign-posting and engineering assistance, and many other demands brought on by a nation at war. Club executives visited military camps to plan route sign-posts and maps. Many Army divisions were training in southern California and G.I.s were everywhere.

The Club was apprehensive that rationing would cut down memberships and the need for motoring services. During the war no new cars were to be produced, and the Club anticipated few motorists on the road. No one could predict when the war would end, of course. Yet, despite such travails and dangers, Club membership was to continue to burgeon. In 1939, the Club rolls boasted 121,808. The climb was steady. By 1945, membership had risen to 204,584, indicative of the vital role of automotive transportation during the war years.

In a matter of days after Pearl Harbor, a freeze was ordered on the sale of tires and tubes, followed later by strict rationing. By the next month, production of new autos for civilian use was stopped, and there was even a panicky proposal in the U. S. Senate that civilian autos be confiscated.

Meanwhile, the Club pushed remedial proposals of its own. One was to reduce speed limits to get maximum usage from autos and tires, as well as save gas. "Keep it under 40" was the slogan. President Roosevelt asked governors of all the states to cooperate and, later, the Office of

PLATE 96 *The Club joined the nation in its vigorous defense activity. G.I.s were everywhere now, often without transportation, and the Club's Service Motor Corps urged the motorist to "Give them a Lift." Other campaigns: sign-posting military camps, mapping emergency landing fields, selling Defense Saving Stamps, training Red Cross Motor Corps units, rationing tires and gas, and, for the first time, discouraging motoring.*

Defense Transportation was to declare a maximum limit for autos of 35 mph.

Various other moves were geared to the war effort. The Club started safety driving schools for drivers of military vehicles and training courses for Red Cross Motor Corps units. By January, 1942, the Wartime Motoring Information Bureau was a hive of activity, with the Club explaining to members the sometimes confusing new wartime measures and rationing requirements. Too, in a few months, 15,000 copies of a guide to wartime auto care, *Keep 'Em Rolling,* were distributed by the Club.

In that spring of 1942, the five-point "Drive for Victory!" program was started with other organizations to help save tires and autos. It called for pledges by motorists to drive under 40 mph, drive as little as possible, share autos, have periodic inspections, and cooperate in staggering business hours to relieve congestion. With this came the Rubber Salvage Drive in which the Club handled more than 80,000 pounds of discarded tires.

Yet, even as they aided the federal government at every turn, Club directors looked carefully at each request in those early days of excitement which, at times, reached almost hysterical limits. For example, one of the first rationing suggestions was so extreme it would have brought chaos to the state's entire economy, as well as all war industries in southern California. The Federal Office of Price Administration had cut gas supplies drastically on the East Coast and in the South because of the problems involved in transporting fuel to these areas. Yet on the Pacific Coast, where gasoline was being produced, there was no real shortage in the early days of the war. The OPA, however, took a moral stand. They felt the whole nation should "sacrifice." The Club pointed out that the West not only lacked the mass transportation facilities of the East, but distances were much greater for the average Westerner. The result was the West was given an equitable allowance of ration cards.

With such radical changes in national problems, the Club had to make equally radical adjustments in various ways. President Bauer, in defining this new role, noted in the annual report for 1943: "Whereas for 40 years the Club has taken the lead in encouraging the volume and radius of travel for business and recreation, it became necessary almost overnight to discourage all but essential motoring."

Meanwhile, internally, the Club faced other problems. As of December,

PLATE 97 *Immediately after Pearl Harbor, tires were first not sold at all, and then were strictly rationed. The Auto Club launched its "Drive for Victory" campaign in 1942 to promote care of tires and cars for longer use, and forty tons of rubber were gathered in the "Rubber Salvage Drive."*

PLATE *98 The end of the war brought with it the great joy of watching gas ration coupons go up in smoke. And once again, motorists could buy a new car, go faster than 35 mph and have the luxury of a Sunday afternoon drive.*

1944, a total of 201 employees had gone into military service. "News from Home," a mimeographed monthly bulletin, kept them up on Club doings.

Pearl Harbor had found a seasoned array of men on the board. They were Harry Bauer, Henry Keller, Horace Miller, Alexander Macbeth, Henry MacKay, Jr., George Wallace, Harry Chandler, W. L. Valentine and Stuart O'Melveny. All were not only versed in Club concerns but also deeply immersed in the life of the city as civic and business leaders.

The Club ran into a roadblock in one of its initial moves to aid the war effort. On January 8, J. Allen Davis asked California's Governor Olson to open a call for a special session of the legislature to consider reducing the state speed limit from 55 mph to 45 mph to conserve tires, gas and autos. The governor refused, explaining that he had refused other requests and didn't want to keep the legislature in session longer than necessary. Davis and Phil Hanna, WESTWAYS' editor, then hit upon an alternate idea which they suggested to the directors: an unofficial campaign of persuasion and education with the northern club to convince the public of the need for driving slower. It was to be the beginning of the "Keep It Under 40" program.

Related directly to the war, also, was the prohibition on new cars. There had been 207,715 policies written by the Exchange and Bureau in 1941. But since there were no new car sales, there would be little if any new insurance written. Even though premium rates on collision and property damage would be raised immediately, the future seemed uncertain.

Meanwhile, other vigorous campaigns, born of war needs, were under way. WESTWAYS' articles dealt with such subjects as blackouts and driving. The Service Motor Corps explained the need for slow driving and the use of metal strips on license plates to conserve a million and a half pounds of steel. The Corps promoted a stepchild of the tire business—retreading and recapping—which had suddenly emerged from being a despised intrusion on tire sales to a patriotic venture in conservation. It also dealt with basic car care, something which many motorists had forgotten since the days when the auto was an avocation—a luxury item for hobbyists.

All Club offices were selling Defense Saving Stamps by then, and the Club also supplied in the first months of the war some 30,000 maps to the armed forces. The Club was selling the new federal Auto Use stamps, had bought five new trucks to keep up with sign-posting work and started a new service—the Wartime Motoring Information Bureau.

President Roosevelt soon did what California's governor hadn't done for the Club—establish a uniform national speed limit by executive order. Yet the Club clashed with the federal government on another matter at about the same time. It protested to Congress a proposal to exempt defense contractors from state gasoline tax. The definition of a defense contractor was so loosely drawn, the Club maintained, that there would be a serious decline in state gas tax revenue which would jeopardize highway and road maintenance.

Local problems related to the war effort also had to be considered. One Los Angeles city proposal which the Club opposed called for using traffic fines for ornamental street light standards; also, the advocates of the parking meter were back at work again with the Club opposing them.

The Club, meanwhile, had sold 83,009 auto stamps, taking pressure off the frantic Post Office Department. The board of governors also authorized the purchase of U.S. treasury certificates not to exceed $100,-000.

The International Pacific Highway project moved slowly on. Mexico borrowed $30 million from the U.S., and expectations in the spring of 1942 were that the highway would be completed by 1943. But it was far from that simple. Within Mexico there was great political pressure to divert the borrowed funds to lateral roads and to improve railways. By winter there was practically no construction on the highway. But, in June, 1943, the Club received a report that the Central American portion was passable by Army vehicles except for a 150-mile stretch between Panama and Costa Rica. By fall, 1943, however, the Army engineers lost all interest in the project, originally being pushed to protect the Panama Canal. The engineers had their hands full in North Africa, so the work was turned over to the Bureau of Public Roads which had limited money for such work. The project bogged until a chaotic windstorm in Mazatlán made the President of Mexico realize the need for better communications. He asked for immediate action on the west coast highway. The Club was asked to advance funds to set up offices in Mexico to further the work but it refused. It did agree, however, to pay $3,000, as it had originally proposed for improvement of the highway. But the progress on the project was to continue through war's end to be disappointing and slow.

To the Club, California's highways, roads and motorists' needs were keener during those years of shortages of men, material and funds. Directors approved plans for a postwar rehabilitation bond issue for highways and opposed a change in the gas tax during the 1943 legislative session. A variety of other bills were of importance that year, including one to reorganize the State Highway Commission to seven members and to appropriate $12 million from the general fund for highway surveys and acquisition of rights-of-way after the war.

The Club continued to look at the prospects for new freeways in southern California. The general plan for postwar freeway construction proposed by the Club was a statewide trunk line, including routes within cities as well as a state metropolitan system. The plan was to be financed by increasing the gas tax. (This concept later materialized after great difficulty and included 12,000 miles of freeways costing more than $10 billion.)

An unhappy event occurred in May, 1942—the death of Director William L. Valentine, a pioneer oilman who had founded the city of San Marino. He had served as a director since 1910, having been Club president from 1921 to 1926. He was to be replaced by Neil Petree. Other deaths were to follow. Allen Balch, who had been a director from 1911 to 1939, died in April, 1943, and Los Angeles *Times* publisher, Harry Chandler, who had served as a director from 1913 to 1944, died a year later.

Another formidable project, the Alaska Coast Highway, appeared to be unsettled in 1942. The Club received reports that the Federal Works Agency was losing interest. In the years to follow, progress was watched closely by the Club. An inland route to Fairbanks for government vehicles was opened on November 20, 1942. But the additional route "A" of the Alaska Highway, called for in the Diamond Bill, was disapproved by the Agency a short time later. In 1934, the engineer in charge of the military highway wrote E. E. East, the Club's chief engineer, on the matter of connecting Prince George with the Alaska Highway, asking the Club to encourage the idea. This link was constructed.

Meanwhile, a variety of war-created problems merited attention. The Club was concerned over tires, which were being bought as scrap for twenty cents each by the government's Defense Supplies Corporation, while they were actually appraised as worth $14 or more by Club staffers. The DSC claimed lack of manpower to make accurate appraisals.

The Club purchased $5 million in war damage insurance for $375 to protect Exchange securities in the bank vaults. There was still the threat of attack from Japan. Yet even as it planned for such unlikely crisis, it looked ahead with a Postwar Planning committee made up of staffers.

New demands and problems emerged as the Allies turned the tide of the war. Tires had been rationed, followed by autos, then gasoline. Auto parts for civilians became more difficult to obtain with each passing month, and such nonessential elements as fenders, radiator grills and running boards weren't even produced. Mechanics were in short supply. In the first four months of 1943, there was a net loss of 637 Club members resulting from such woes.

WESTWAYS was to suffer a decline in readers because paper rationing dictated a reduction in magazine size. Even though Service Patrol activities were cut, the men continued to aid more than 11,000 motorists during 1943. The Touring Bureau made twenty-two charting trips for the Army and issued 2,596,835 maps, while 9,810 temporary and 6,365 permanent signs were erected. The Club's map activities were turned toward military work that included eighty special maps for the armed forces. Too, 7,468 large blue-line maps and 156,673 regular maps were issued, which freed military engineers for overseas duty. By March, 1944, Club membership had made a steady climb back and was at an all-time high of 152,594. It was to continue up and up, and by November of that year it was 170,208.

As 1945 began the Allied victory seemed assured. A world at war had learned to live and adjust. The Club had come through with flying colors, giving service to the military as well as its own members.

It seemed that an organization which had weathered the Depression and World War II with such enterprise could face any problem that the future might pose.

A new era was just over the horizon. With war's end was to come the happy crisis of booming growth in southern California.

Chapter 15

JOHNNY COMES DRIVING HOME AGAIN

"I would fail in my duty if I did not make of record my appreciation of the initiative, resourcefulness and aggressive action displayed by the personnel of your organization engaged in this work, and the part the results of their action played in the efficient and effective prosecution of the war effort."

—Letter to Club President Harry J. Bauer,
from Lieutenant General John L. DeWitt,
Commander of the Western Defense Command,
October 25, 1945.

As WORLD WAR II did not *really* begin with a shocking and un-expected suddenness, neither did it end with an abrupt finale.

It seemed obvious that our victory was assured by the beginning of 1945. But it was a brutal and trying year: the Allies invaded Germany. President Roosevelt died. The Nazis surrendered in May. In August, the atom bomb was dropped on Hiroshima. Japan surrendered a week later.

The nation was, by now, so accustomed to the war that it had to face a new, albeit happier, crisis. Everywhere the word "adjustment" was in vogue. Returning servicemen had to adjust to civilian life. Businesses had to readjust to peacetime selling, and industry to production changes.

The auto industry had to turn its sights to the long-range future once again and dream of what would attract and fascinate the American motorist five years ahead.

At the Club, the year 1945 brought the same problems the rest of America faced. It not only had to look to the future and surmise what was to come, it also had to look back over the past hard-working years of improvising and use them as a guide.

By 1945, the Club's war record was tallied amidst the frantic pace. Map making had been a particularly busy war activity for the Club. As of August, 224,799 maps had been issued to the Army and Navy, National Guard, peace officers and civilian defense groups at a cost to the Club of $32,503.43. Club staffers worked constantly with the military, revising maps to meet special needs. A three-man team—cartographer, draftsman and driver—made up the usual Club field crew, touring southern California in an auto and trailer on field trips. Their information was later put into final form at the Club headquarters. Typical of the special maps made during the period were: a large relief map of the Southern California Sector of the Western Defense Command; crash maps of a forty-mile area for the Air Ferry Command; 527 maps for military officers showing the location of all military and naval installations in the U.S. with index books; off-shore relief maps of the Channel Islands; emergency landing-field maps showing railroads, telephone lines and major highways; large blue-line maps of special areas. By war's end, Club cars had traveled

325,389 miles accomplishing these chores with the Club picking up the tab.

A similarly impressive record was tabulated by the sign-posting department. The field secretary reported: "As a result of the offer made to the Commanding General of the Ninth Service Command in June, 1941, the Club's signposting department has been called upon by nearly all major military and naval establishments in Southern California. . . ." Club staffers assisted in plotting traffic control, warning signals and the like in these military posts. With the dimout regulation they put up some 2,400 "dimout" and "turn-on" permanent signs, as well as 5,000 temporary ones. By August, 1945, the department had put up nearly 24,000 such signs, spending 70 percent of its time at such war activity, traveling 176,514 miles in the process.

As the result of such voluntary war work, at an estimated cost of more than $250,000, there were literally hundreds of citations and letters of thanks. The Commandant of the 11th Naval District presented the Club with the U. S. Navy citation of Meritorious Wartime Service. The Office of Price Administration praised Club assistance, General H. H. "Hap" Arnold signed a citation from the Air Force, the Commanding General of the Western Defense Command presented the Club with a Certificate of Appreciation at ceremonies at Fort MacArthur.

A variety of government rulings changed Club policies. It could not issue membership or insurance to Japanese nationals (as distinct from Japanese-American citizens) under the Trading With the Enemy Act. The Anti-Inflation Act of 1942 had curbed an array of Club policies on prices, wages and salaries (as it did with other firms and organizations), and the Club had to obtain authorization to buy sign equipment and paper for WESTWAYS. The Club could not hire new employees without authorization, had to apply for salary increases, and faced hundreds of other specific regulations. The wartime excess profits tax required the Club, like others, to pay taxes to a peak of 90 percent of earnings during several war years. Despite such a maze of needed rules and changes in the wartime economy, the Club had, nevertheless, stayed intact and grown.

A loss of directors—the old guard who had so cautiously guided Club destiny over the years—continued to plague the organization during the latter half of the forties. Alexander Macbeth, a director for fifteen years, died in 1945, and Henry MacKay, Jr., with eleven years as a director, was forced to resign due to ill health in 1946. Henry W. Keller, the second vice president, resigned in 1949 after 40 years' service.

But new leaders emerged. Edward R. Valentine was elected a director in 1945 to replace Harry Chandler who had died the year before. Asa V. Call, Claiborn A. Saint and Knox Farrand came on as directors in the next few years. Harry Bauer served as president during all these years. In addition to directors, a number of valued staff members died during the same five years. They included: Douglass Rhodes, manager of the sign-posting department; E. B. Lefferts, manager of public safety; Edwin Pederson, assistant field manager; D. C. Mitchell, assistant manager of the Interinsurance Exchange; Carl E. McStay, field secretary, who retired to an advisory capacity and died soon after.

Drastically hit had been the Finance Department during those war years. No autos for civilian use were produced for three and a half years, and the 1942 models had been strictly rationed. Federal limitations had compounded the shortage: there were the twenty-four-month contracts to finance autos, first introduced in 1939, but later cut back to an eighteen-month limitation with a full one-third down payment upon purchase. Added to this was the Soldiers and Sailors Moritorium Act, excusing those in military service, if need be, from payments.

Within two years after Pearl Harbor, demands on the Finance Department had all but vanished. Typically, records show, no single contract was issued in November, 1944, and those contracts in force added up to less than $5,000. In January, 1942, less than two years before, there were 8,679 contracts totaling more than three and a half million dollars in force. There were just no cars to buy. It was not until June, 1946, that auto manufacturers could again start producing for civilians.

The Club during these years maintained its policy of financing only new cars. This meant fewer contracts but, also, fewer losses. Still, the department was to recover to limits past the wildest dreams in the burgeoning postwar period. By 1950 contracts were to number 10,186. That year staffers made a summation of the twenty-year history of the department. It showed 71,803 contracts had been issued for a total amount of more than $63 million. Remarkably, total losses in bad contracts to members was 4/1000 of one percent, or $2,658. The directors' policy of utmost conservatism in financing had paid off for Club members.

If lack of new autos created havoc, the survival of the old had created its own special troubles. By 1945, thousands of autos were hung together with spit and a prayer which, as expected, led to more and more accidents, claims for injury and damage. In June, 1945, a survey showed the Insurance Exchange could expect a loss of more than a million dollars in twenty-four months due to low rates and added claims. The Exchange could anticipate further problems if it continued to grant an original discount (as compared to Board rates of 15 percent and 20 percent) on certain collision premiums, and if it continued to make a return of 15 percent on original premium deposits.

The next month original discounts were discontinued on new and renewal policies and return premium rates cut from 15 to 10 percent starting August, 1945. Still, it wasn't enough to cut the net loss, and war's end added to the crisis. For gas rationing ended the same month as did the 35 mph speed limit. Speed-hungry and scenery-starved members' enthusiasm led to more accidents and new claims. The report from the year showed more policies and premiums, but an underwriting loss of $188,196. A variety of causes could be found. Lack of new parts, no new cars, low insurance rates, increased speed limits, too many autos for safe driving—all took their toll. Desperate measures were in order. No savings return on policies was one taken in August of 1946. Another was no discounts, except the 15 percent on collision premiums on new autos.

Even then there seemed no real solution. For the study for 1946 showed an underwriting loss of some $3 million to Standard Accident Insurance Co., allied with the Exchange. Hopefully, a change for the better would come with a new concept. In February, 1947, there was an increase of 25 percent in bodily injury liability rates and 30 percent in property damage liability. By June of 1947 the loss ratio for the year was about 42 percent, and it was estimated that by the end of July the Exchange would be back to its old position of strength. The tide had turned.

The ancient autos and speed-happy motorists disappeared slowly. By July, 1948, it was possible to reinstate a return of 10 percent premium deposit on most policies. By December, the return on premium deposit, amounting to 20 percent, was made on policies expiring after March 1, 1949. The rate was increased to 30 percent in 1950, thanks to fewer accidents, but cut back to 20 percent again that December. The lesson was clear. Insurance could change more quickly from loss to profit and back again than any other business known. Answer: be conservative.

Meanwhile, the insurance business was adjusting to the postwar era legislation. Senate Bill 1572 was passed in 1947 providing for insurance rating bureaus to meet a U. S. Supreme Court decision. The high court had called for appropriate state laws to assure fair rates, and thus make federal legislation unnecessary. (An insurance carrier could join a rating bureau, but didn't have to do so.) Another bill established an assigned risk plan for all car insurance carriers, while the Financial Responsibility

PLATE 99   *The Club's 50th birthday party was another time to celebrate. The mayor proclaimed "Auto Club Week," Standish L. Mitchell cut the cake, Arthur Van de Camp (second from right) donated it, and employees ate it. The paternal Mr. Mitchell directed Auto Club activity for over forty years.*

Act of 1929 was greatly expanded to insure payment of traffic accident claims.

For years the Automobile Club of Southern California and the American Automobile Association had had their differences. The Club and AAA had been affiliated from 1903 to 1915, then broke abruptly in a quarrel over the matter of sanctioning auto racing in southern California. For thirty years the AAA had intermittently tried to mend the relationship, sometimes by pleading and, unhappily, sometimes by threat. Club directors had refused.

But, by the postwar period, there had been leadership changes and the climate warmed considerably. In August, 1945, the AAA made another offer of rapprochement. The Club and the directors agreed to ponder it. In November, the directors sent the Club's general manager, Standish Mitchell, and general counsel J. Allen Davis to Washington, D.C., AAA headquarters, to look into the AAA operations. In January, 1946, they recommended re-affiliation, and the following December directors voted 6-to-1 in favor. It was clearly understood that the Club would retain its autonomy and independently administer its own services to members as an affiliated Club. But it was clearly to the Club's advantage of offering better service. With members motoring into other areas in increasing numbers, a reciprocal service under AAA affiliation was the most advantageous course. In addition, the AAA was an on-the-scene voice in the nation's capital to speak for motorists' needs. The old wounds had been healed. Harry J. Bauer joined the AAA board of directors and executive committee in 1947.

Meanwhile, the staff was busy with an array of other activities during those busy postwar years. And the interests of the Club sometimes reached past motoring issues proper into secondary fields. For example, C. B. Harrison, manager of the Outing Bureau, was seriously concerned about the effects of the population growth in California on hunting and fishing. Between 1940 and 1946 some 2,643,340 new Californians had appeared. Result: state agencies were spending $8 million a year to provide fish and game. Many streams had disappeared and the question of where to plant fish was a ticklish one.

The Public Safety Department, too, had its own worries. Traffic had burgeoned in Los Angeles above all expectations during the postwar years. There was only the Pasadena Freeway to alleviate the spreading congestion. In 1948 the mayor asked the Club, the Los Angeles Traffic Association and the Automotive Safety Foundation of Washington, D.C., to loan engineers for a survey committee.

Six months later the mayor received a comprehensive report which discussed traffic in terms of importance, history and growth, special elements of the problem, duties of government agencies and non-government agencies, essential functions of traffic management and, finally, conclusions and recommendations. It called for creation of a five-man traffic commission, a department of traffic engineering and a technical coordinating committee made up of various city officials. It also called for various charter amendments. The city council and mayor put some recommendations into effect and two members, Joseph E. Havenner, then manager of the Club's Public Safety Department, and D. Grant Mickle, director of the traffic engineer division of the Automotive Safety Foundation, were asked to make additional reports. One, due in 1952, was to review the three years of progress and analyze deficiencies left over from the 1948 report. The other was a special survey to be made in 1955, reporting on achievements and remaining needs.

Highway legislation was, of course, a major issue after the war years. The plans for a postwar trunk system of freeways to be built through increased gas tax had been suggested to the Board by Ernest East in 1943. In early 1944, the Club had joined with the northern Club and other groups in establishing a committee to promote freeways. In November of that year the State Division of Highways had prepared a report for the legislature pointing up the desperate needs for highways and the importance of increasing expenditures. The program called for spending $680 million in the first ten years. Existing revenue rates could provide far less than needed.

The California Major Highway Development Committee developed measures which were introduced in the legislature in January, 1945. The proposals called for a statewide system of limited access highways or freeways—600 miles in cities, 3,300 miles in rural areas—to be financed by increasing the gas tax from 3 to 4½ cents per gallon.

Trouble appeared almost immediately. The legislature, President Bauer told directors, didn't seem likely to approve the tax increase. By March, directors were told that a majority in both the Senate and Assembly were opposed to the gas tax increase; strong pressure was being exerted to restore prior cuts in the sales tax, bank and corporation taxes and personal income taxes to create a $100 million postwar fund. This money, according to the plan, would be distributed to counties and cities for construction purposes, including roads and streets.

The committee lost the day. The proposed 1945 measures were defeated.

At the end of the legislative session it was obvious a more complete study of highway problems was needed. The Club and other interested parties supported Senate Concurrent Resolution No. 27, introduced by Senator Randolph Collier, calling for a joint fact-finding committee. This group later appointed an advisory committee made up of both unofficial and official parties. Actively involved in the study was Club director Neil Petree, who had been appointed chairman of the highway committee of the Los Angeles Chamber of Commerce. He reported progress regularly at Club board meetings, and in March of 1946 he told directors of the program for an April meeting of a joint legislative committee to study proposed highway legislation. This legislative group held conferences with a wide array of interested parties and presented a final tentative report with twenty-four recommendations in December, 1946. That same month Petree was made a member of the California Major Highway Development Committee, on which East and J. Allen Davis had been members since its inception in 1944.

The stage was set for the next effort in the legislative session of 1947.

The Collier-Burns measure called for an expanded highway program and a 1½-cent increase in the gas tax. The Club appropriated $20,000 for the campaign and strong support came from other agencies which made up the California Major Highway Development Committee, as well as other civic groups. Governor Warren and other state highway officials also supported the program.

The bill was introduced in the legislature in January, 1947. Six months of controversy and debate followed, but it finally passed the legislature as Senate Bill No. 5 in June. It included: the 1½-cent increase in gas tax; the same increase for diesel fuel; a registration fee increase from $3.00 to $6.00; an increase in operators' and chauffeurs' license fees; increased taxes on commercial vehicles.

Estimate was that the Collier-Burns Highway Act would bring in $175 million the first year, approximately $70 million more than would have been collected under old statutes. It called for a distribution of state highway construction funds of 45 percent in the north and 55 percent in the south and increased monies to counties and cities. Noted President Bauer: ". . . In the years to come, 1947 will be remembered as a memorable year in California's motoring history because we are now moving toward the development of facilities over which the motoring public may move with greater rapidity and safety." He could have added, "And just in time!"

The added revenue hastened construction of the Hollywood, Santa Ana and Harbor freeways during the period to December 31, 1950.

Still, a new problem had come, too, with southern California's booming popularity—smog. By the end of the war, the haze that shrouded the Los Angeles basin had become a growing nuisance. In 1945, the Club had started an investigation. Uniform smoke abatement laws in 1946 helped some, as did the building of eleven incinerators to end open-dump burning.

In 1947 the California State Legislature passed Assembly Bill 1, a pioneer measure which empowered county boards of supervisors to create local agencies with the authority to control air pollution in its county.

On October 14, 1947, the Los Angeles County Board of Supervisors established an Air Pollution Control District (APCD), and the fight against smog entered a new phase, with the Club a major participant in the campaign.

By December, 1950, the Club was involved in a happier affair. December 13 marked its 50th anniversary. The week was proclaimed "Auto Club Week" by Mayor Bowron. The Advertising Club of Los Angeles gave a luncheon to celebrate the event. An array of firms and groups—the B. F. Goodrich Co., Van de Kamp's Bakeries, General Petroleum, the Horseless Carriage Club—joined in the festivities with special gifts and events. A parade of thirty-seven ancient autos made its way in a cavalcade re-enacting the Club's inter-city reliability run of 1906. Letters of congratulations and praise poured in from Governor Earl Warren, Donald W. Douglas, president of the Douglas Aircraft Company, Robert G. Sproul, president of the University of California, J. E. Wallace Sterling, president of Stanford University and many, many others.

It was all a far, far cry from that distant day when the city was a pastoral town and membership in the Club just ten. In 1939 membership had been 121,808. By 1950 it was 306,302, an increase of 184,494.

During the crisis of war, with its rationing, lack of new autos and re-stricting regulations, the Club had grown with startling speed.

As for the population of California, the statistics were even more re-markable. In the summer of 1900 there had been 1,485,053 Cali-fornians. By 1940 this had climbed steadily to 6,907,387. The next decade saw some 3,500,000 more added to the census rolls. It seemed that some sort of tapering off was ahead. Little did the average motorist know that there was no end in sight, and that the population would soar, bringing also a fantastic number of new drivers on the road each year.

Chapter 16

BEGINNING THE SECOND FIFTY YEARS

"If you can't stand the heat, stay out of the kitchen."

—Harry Truman

THERE WAS HEAT aplenty for everyone when the Club began its second half-century. The national atmosphere was one of tension and concern. While the major topic of conversation across the land was politics and presidential candidates, America's greatest problems were economic and military.

The inflationary spiral seemed endless as costs continued to climb along with wages in the familiar pattern. Much of the public was disheartened and depressed by the Korean War which seemed to be in a hopeless stalemate. Stopping the spread of Communism appeared an endless mission for a whole generation of Americans with no end in sight—except the possible horror of atomic war.

Still, all was not dismal. The U.S. economy had proved itself full of an equally endless vitality. Despite defense work, there was very little shortage of consumer goods. Farmers had successfully weathered a devastating drought and turned in the third biggest harvest in history. U.S. industry was employing a record-breaking 62,570,000 people.

Amidst the uproar over budget and taxes, the U.S. had re-armed, after the drastic slicing that followed World War II. America's defensive posture was at its highest peak since then, even while the perplexing issue was just how many world-wide problems the U.S. taxpayer could carry.

Lesser and happier events marched on. Sports fans concerned themselves with the Olympics at Helsinki. There were high hopes for a polio vaccine. "I Love Lucy" was sweeping the television rating game with 30 million viewers. The Viking rocket was probing the skies, the forerunner of the great weapons to come.

The auto industry had its own special woes, feeling the pinch of some shortages, unlike most of America. In 1952, the government placed some tooling restrictions on automakers. Despite this, and material shortages too, the industry turned out designs using more and more chrome trim. Copper shortages also called for thinner ignition wiring, and a steel strike forced some assembly plants to close down.

Yet progress was made in the face of such impediments. There were better carburetors and manifolds that year, and the overhead-valve V-type motor came into its own. Compacts were unveiled and Ford offered both a new body design and a six-cylinder engine—a major change from the old standby, the V-8. Two new Lincolns, the Capri and Cosmopolitan, emerged, part of a multi-million dollar re-tooling move aimed at combating Cadillac and Chrysler. Willys-Overland reappeared after a decade's absence as a passenger car with a six-cylinder, 35-mile-per-gallon car, the Aero. Yet "low priced" cars were nearly a memory. All cost only slightly less than lower priced Fords and Chevrolets.

Car ownership reached an all-time high that year with some 52 million passenger cars which annually used 38 billion gallons of gasoline. California, with about five million cars, ranked first in auto registrations. Only Cadillacs were in short supply in 1952, with most dealers quoting an eight-month delay due to defense work by the firm.

Two new automotive innovations came in 1952. Power brakes were standard equipment on some of the bigger autos, and Oldsmobile offered a headlight dimmer which was operated automatically by the lights of an on-coming car. The latter gadget was not to catch on, but it proved a harbinger of the electronic complexities to come.

By 1953 a new craze was sweeping the U.S. motoring scene. The zooming, hard-riding sports car made in Europe was to be seen in ever-increasing numbers. Why? Perhaps the U.S. automaker had reached too far in offering comfort and ease. To thousands of Americans, particularly the young, the thrill of shifting, braking and cornering as Barney Oldfield had once done returned motoring from a comfortable, dull task to a sport once again.

The MG and Jaguar became a commonplace sight, while the costly and still rare Ferrari (up to $15,000) continued to attract crowds of admirers when parked on a city street. Some 30,000 foreign cars had been sold in 1952 in the U.S. The sales graph continued to climb in 1953.

The U.S. auto industry started to turn out some light cars. Or at least experiment with them even while "Detroit irons," as the sports car fans scornfully dubbed them, continued to get bigger and more luxurious. Oldsmobile offered Frigidaire air-conditioning. Hydraulically operated front seats became common and sixteen makes of popular autos added automatic transmissions.

The horsepower race went on with Cadillac leading at 210 and Lincoln close behind at 205. The V-8 engine was still the most popular. Many companies started to experiment with Fiberglas bodies. Chevrolet cautiously tested the market with 300 sports car-oriented Corvettes and Kaiser-Frazer offered the DKF, only thirty-six inches high, to appeal to the racing fan.

It was also a milestone year. Ford celebrated its 50th anniversary and Studebaker its 100th in 1953. Too, a statistician came up with a significant, if useless, figure that year. There were enough autos on the road to carry the entire U.S. population at once.

The Club began its second fifty years with a sophistication born of the bitter Depression years, the war years, and the continuing effort to maintain and build membership in the face of both. Each crisis had taught its own lesson. When membership had fallen to 77,000 in 1934 the Club had taken a fresh look to refine services and add activities to attract new members. The war years had forced the Club to adapt to critical shortages and concentrate its efforts and resources where the most good could be accomplished. By the end of 1950 membership had grown to 306,000.

Now it faced a new crisis. The future had seemed bright enough. Those who dabble with charts and graphs predicted a remarkable population growth ahead. But they were too conservative. In April, 1950, for example, the population of the fifteen southern California counties served by the Club stood at 6,418,295. In a decade this was to leap to more than 10 million. Metropolitan Los Angeles itself was to grow from 4,151,687 to more than six million. Auto registration in California was to climb between 1950 and 1957 from some five million to nearly seven and a half million.

All earlier predictions had been too cautious. In the days when the Club started and there were 102,478 Angelenos, "starry-eyed dreamers" said the area would someday have a million people. The boosters of mid-century proved equally conservative.

The discrepancies were quickly apparent to Club directors. There was a desperate need for more and better district offices. As pressures grew, the Club established a real estate department to manage the expansion needs. The bustling growth had made it more and more difficult to lease good space in proper locations. A new policy was started in 1956. The Club began to buy land and build district offices, leasing only when conditions were right. By 1957 the Club had built five such facilities and leased a number of new buildings to meet the growing needs.

Highways were a more paramount concern for the Club as traffic swelled on California's roadways. A half century before the ten founders of the Club had stated their purpose was "to promote the construction, improvement and maintenance of good roads." Their dream had been a few unrutted bypaths where they could chug along at ten miles an hour. The first paved road in California was not to come until 1912.

How mystified and bemused they would have been to see their original campaign for better roads as it was to be conducted a half century later! For now great concrete and steel freeways, designed to carry thousands of autos each hour in an endless stream, were the concern of those who had inherited their mission. Unlike the founders who had pleaded their cause with city fathers over a five-cent mug of beer and free lunch, Club spokesmen now labored their way through the intricacies of bills and proposals in the busy legislative halls of Sacramento.

In 1951 a powerful coalition was formed to fight for better highways. The California Major Highways Development Committee was reactivated with five participating groups—the Club, the California State Automobile Association, the California State Chamber of Commerce, the County Supervisors Association of California and the League of California Cities, (Club director Neil Petree served as first chairman until he was elected president of the California State Chamber of Commerce in 1952.) The 1947 Collier-Burns Act had increased highway revenues to accelerate freeway construction. This stepped-up building program generated opposition in some areas. As always, there were those interests who wanted to raid the highway treasury for other causes. Too, in the years following the 1947 Act, the general public had come to take for granted that the systems would be completed without a hitch. The Committee set out to win the day and sell the freeway program in California.

It was a complex assignment. The increase in revenues under the Collier-Burns Act of 1947 was nowhere near enough to meet the burgeoning needs of the state with its booming population and the inadequate roads which resulted from the decline in road building during World War II.

Before the 1951 legislative session, State Senator Randolph Collier asked the Division of Highways to make a survey to see where the state stood. The results were startling. The survey showed that in January, 1951, total deficiencies were more than three billion dollars and that some 80 percent of the 11,000 miles of state highways were inadequate to meet present and future traffic needs. Estimated revenue from current sources, the Club's E. E. East estimated, would be only $1,441,000,000 between 1952 and 1962 for construction and highway right-of-way acquisition. Immediate action was imperative.

The problem facing politicians and the Club was how best to solve the dilemma. Several legislative sessions were to struggle for an answer, including proposed bond issues of some one billion dollars to provide immediate funds, with the payment of principal and interest coming from future gas tax revenue with an additional two cent increase. The Committee opposed this.

The solution came in the Lincoln Highway Bill of 1953. It increased the gas tax from 4½ to 6 cents and the diesel fuel tax from 4½ to 7 cents. It increased other highway user taxes a proportionate 33 percent, with the exception of the 3 percent gross receipts tax on "for hire" trucks and buses. It was to be a ten year program to develop the state highway system. Although it provided for a partial reduction at the end of two years in the rate of highway user taxes, later legislative actions maintained the same rates.

The U. S. Congress, too, was to increase the federal gasoline tax steadily during those years. In 1951 it went from 1½ to 2 cents per gallon. An increase to 3 cents came in 1956 when Congress authorized the creation of the remarkable Interstate System, which called for the building of 41,000 miles in new interconnecting superhighways across the nation. New federal gas and highway user taxes went into a special Highway Trust Fund, from which they were redistributed to the states as local construction of the federal highway system progressed.

The Interstate System was to become the backbone for California's own highway system, and it provided a remedy for the nation's obsolete and inadequate network of highways which manifested itself in crisis proportions during the 1950s. All the nation—and most particularly the motorist —were to benefit from the continuing construction of the Interstate System.

California's annual revenue for streets and highways was about $208 million in 1952–53. By 1956–57 this had climbed to more than $424 million and, by 1958–59, was over $525 million. This amount did not include city and county taxes allocated to street and highway work.

Yet even as California struggled with its badly needed highway program, there were the usual efforts in the legislature to raid highway revenues for

PLATE *100 Downtown Los Angeles on a clear day, when not suffering from a tem-*
perature inversion.

other purposes. In 1954, for example, a constitutional amendment (later
defeated) called for gas tax and motor vehicle funds to be spent on off-
street parking facilities. Another move came in 1956 when a group of Bay
Area senators introduced a constitutional amendment calling for gas tax
funds to be diverted to buy rights-of-way for a rapid transit system for their
area. The Club was one of many organizations that fought the move. It
would have meant a major increase in the gas tax, along with cutting
back on the highway development program. Fortunately, a majority of

PLATE *101 Smog came as a real problem to Los Angeles in the late forties. A peculiar climatological condition, the temperature inversion serves as a lid to keep pollutants near the surface. Half of City Hall shows here above a 300-foot temperature inversion.*

the Senate Transportation Committee also opposed the idea and rejected it.

Similar proposals to divert gas tax funds to mass transit were to come in 1957 and 1959. They, too, were defeated. The Club's policy remained that, while it was not opposed to mass transit as such, it was opposed to raiding highways funds to finance such projects.

A spectre that first appeared in southern California in the mid-forties now plagued the area. Smog. It had grown from an annoyance to a coined name, from a petty complaint on certain days to an overwhelming concern. The causes were vague, the responsibility shifting. But the auto was among the list of accused. The Club's engineering and legal departments at the director's request collected a vast array of lore, legend, fact and fancy while the public debate swirled over what it was all about. Theories and angry debate as to causes had cropped up everywhere, as did "panaceas."

The Club had the task of being sure that, in the midst of the furor, the motorist would not be victimized. At the same time the Club cooperated in research efforts by making its own facilities available to investigating agencies. The Air Pollution Foundation and meetings of various civic and citizen groups were attended and local legislation was studied by Club staffers. When proposed county legislation on motor vehicles came it often seemed excessively drastic and harsh for motorists—as well as unenforceable. Proposed laws called, for example, for all autos to stop and stay wherever they might be during a second-stage smog alert and for all industry to close down unless they had met certain standards. These laws were later revised.

During those years a vast array of law was proposed and enacted in Sacramento: special license plates were approved in 1951 for "horseless carriages" over 35 years old (used mainly for historical exhibit) and new laws were passed for the loading and securing of lumber, poles and baled hay on trucks. In 1953, the Department of Motor Vehicles took over issuing special plates to ham radio operators and regulations were adopted for driving schools. Traffic courts were required to impose penalty assessments in addition to fines on some convictions.

By 1955, there were new laws for beam headlights, brake performance and safety belt sales while, two years later, each driver's license was required to have a photo of the licensee. New laws governing auto dealers and salesmen were also put into effect, and still more regulations governed transporting explosives.

The Club was involved in this tide of new legislation in sifting the good from the bad, trying to avoid the trivial and detrimental in the welter of ideas to solve highway problems by law. In 1955, for example, 345 bills to amend 240 sections of the Vehicle Code and to add 173 more and repeal 33 sections were introduced in the legislature. Also, thirty-three Vehicle Code sections were up for repeal. The legislature finally amended 120, added seventy and repealed ten. Each had to be scrutinized by the Club for its implications and a position taken which the Club felt was in the best interest of the California motorist.

The Interinsurance Exchange was to make its own way back to solid growth by the beginning of 1951. The days of the high loss ratio of the postwar period, which had been met with increased rates and decreases in original discounts, had passed. A report in September, 1953, pointed up the progress. There had been a 13.2 percent underwriting gain for the seven months of that year as compared with a 4.5 loss for the same period in 1952. Yet it was clear that the auto insurance business was changing. Every possible economy was put into effect. The Standard Accident Insurance Company had carried the substantial risks on liability insurance for Club members in the past, while the Interinsurance Exchange handled only material damages to member's autos. Now, with a growth in the volume of business, a review was made. It was deemed desirable to consolidate the policies, thus passing along savings to policyholders. The Interinsurance Exchange began writing both policies on January 1, 1957. In March, 1956 the directors appointed Ralph L. Inglis to the newly created position of Vice President of Insurance and Manager of the Interinsurance Exchange. Inglis had been president of the Founders Insurance Company for a number of years and was an insurance executive of long experience in the casualty insurance company.

During the early fifties the Club's Public Safety Department conducted a special traffic management study in San Diego, a parking study for Beverly Hills, reviewed the 1952 study for Los Angeles on street management, and completed a comprehensive report on pedestrian accidents. It also held the first Teen-age Traffic Safety Conference and started the High School Safety Economy Runs. All this was in line with a long tradition. Since it was organized in 1921, the department had started many educational programs to improve driver skill and behavior.

It is mortality that ensures historic eras and periods. Both the automobile and the Automobile Club of Southern California were born at the turn of the century. The men who originally staffed the Club were almost uniformly young at the time. Thus, during a short span of time in the fifties, many of the Club's pioneers were lost either through death or retirement. Outstanding among them was Standish L. Mitchell, who came to the

Club in 1911 as Assistant Secretary when there were only some forty employees. He died in 1957, having served his last 21 years as Secretary and General Manager.

This cumulative loss in such a few short years of executive personnel who had worked closely with directors suddenly required new people for leadership positions. Directors, anxious to perpetuate the high grade of Club leadership, developed a plan of reorganization with the assistance of a management consultant firm, McKinsey and Company.

The new plan consolidated several positions and called for an executive vice president responsible for both the Club and Exchange, with six officers directing the various functions. These included a director of administrative services, travel services, field operations, engineering and technical services, general counsel and a vice president for insurance. Other results of the reorganization plan were an expanded budget control program, enlargement of personnel management functions, expansion of field operations functions—including the development of market potential studies, sales training program, and salesmen's compensation plan.

Meanwhile, the re-affiliation with the American Automobile Association in 1947 after the many years of disaffection over early quarrels proved to be most valuable. After the reorganization of the Club, Norman P. Thompson, successor to Standish L. Mitchell and newly appointed executive vice president, expanded the climate of cooperation with the AAA. One palpable benefit of this cooperation was the Club's increased ability to meet the national—and even international—needs of its members.

In the years which followed re-affiliation, the Club was entitled to nominate as directors of the AAA its own Club directors and executive staff, which varied from six to ten in number according to a formula based on membership of all clubs affiliated in the AAA. Between 1947 and 1957, nearly all Club directors and many staff members served as AAA directors, and on several of its important advisory committees. Most prominent among these was Harry Bauer, Club president, who had become a member of the AAA executive committee in 1947 and served until 1960.

For all the accelerated change and trials the early and mid-fifties brought the Club, the organization waxed in prestige and influence. It also grew in numbers, as did the booming population of California. Yet, if Club planners thought the prognosticators of growth had been wrong before, they had still more surprises to come.

Chapter 17

THE CHALLENGE OF GROWTH

"Today, California has 14,445,000 residents and nearly 7,500,000 motor vehicles. The population is expected to be 16,000,000 by 1960 and 20,000,000 by 1970. A corresponding, if not greater, increase in the number of motor vehicles is also expected . . ."

—Annual Report, State Dept. of Public Works, 1957.

W<small>HEN</small> we look at one of those far-out drawings of the world of the future with soaring buttresses and highways connecting at the hundredth-story level, while helicopters flurry about, we take it with more than the proverbial grain of salt. Yet, what would the founders of the Club think if today they were to revisit their once sedate and sleepy town? Would they believe the great churning freeways or the miles of asphalt highways reaching as far as the eye can see?

Indeed, autos themselves have changed so radically that our departed grandfathers probably wouldn't recognize one.

In the 1920s there had been a flamboyant array of body styles—the roadster, touring car, cabriolet, brougham, landaulet and others. By the 1950s the industry had in general settled down to the coupe, sedan, convertible and the popular station wagon as an adjunct to suburban life. Compacts had emerged in ever-increasing numbers and names. Too, the endless race between firms for more extravagant styling went on with emphasis on the clean "continental" look. The first two-seater Thunderbird had come off the line at Ford in 1954, imitative of European sports cars but actually a hybrid prestige car. By 1957 it had become a four-seater and set a trend for the market, grabbing 22 percent of the total sales.

There were other general trends one could observe. A cautious belief born of the show-biz expression, "don't monkey with a hit," permeated the auto industry. Manufacturers followed a success with only a few changes in the next year's model. Aesthetic utility and comfort became the vogue, with automatic shifting, power steering, automatic transmission and limitless electronic refinement. Still another merchandising trend was for firms to offer cars of every size, price and equipment options when possible. The clearcut distinction between low-, medium- and high-priced trade names began to blur as traditionally medium-priced cars started competing for the low-priced market.

In 1958 the frantic pace of burgeoning southern California continued. The Club was trying to stay in stride. Auto registration kept pace with the booming population. By 1960 there were 9,634,936 southern Californians and 8,681,162 registered drivers in the state. Club membership had grown accordingly. Total membership in 1958 was 464,166, and the number continued to soar until by 1965 it reached 752,690. This dramatic increase brought with it certain problems. While caught up in the inflationary spiral, the Club was faced with added capital expenditures and the need for more personnel to assure the continuation of high standards of service to a soaring membership. For fifty years, since 1906, Club dues had remained at $12 a year. Now there was an absolute need to raise them. In 1957 dues were raised to $15 annually, in 1965, they had to be increased once again to $18. There was, however, a reduction in enrollment fee from $3 to $2, and the practice of issuing duplicate cards to man and wife was continued. Additional associate membership cards for children in a family were issued for $6 a year. This increase was essential to keep service at its previous quality and to provide larger facilities to meet membership needs.

The Club was involved almost constantly in new building programs during the early 1960s. The Building Committee approved new building leases, property acquisitions and new construction to meet expanding needs. Only through the concept of the district office did the Club feel it could continue to provide personal service of high quality. By 1965 the Club had either purchased or leased 26 district offices and nearly all rented space had been enlarged. These additions made a total of 65 district offices, and provisions were also made for new offices in the San Fernando Valley and Long Beach.

In 1959 President Harry Bauer declined reelection but agreed to remaining as a director and governor. He had sought to relinquish the presidency for several years prior to this. When he stepped down he recommended that the office be restricted to two terms. Edward Valentine became president next and served in that office until 1961. Valentine, the son of a former director and president, had served as a director since 1945 and as vice president since 1949. His business activities were numerous. He was chairman of the board of the Robinson Building Company, vice president and director of the Fullerton Oil Company, a director and twice president of the California State Chamber of Commerce, a director of the Security First National Bank of Los Angeles, a trustee of the California Institute of Technology and the Huntington Memorial Library.

Clairborne A. Saint, who served as vice president under Valentine, was vice president of R. A. Rowan and Company, Los Angeles' largest real estate firm. He had also been president of the Los Angeles Realty Board, a vice president of the California Real Estate Association, a director of the Merchant and Manufacturers Association, a director of the Children's Hospital Society of Los Angeles and a president of the California Club.

In 1961, another distinguished leader became president: Frank L. King, chairman of the board of directors of Western Bancorporation and United California Bank, as well as vice president of the board of trustees of the University of Southern California.

In 1963, Lloyd Austin took over as Club president. Austin, president of Security First National Bank of Los Angeles, was also a director of Northrup Corporation, Robinson Building Co., Carnation Co., a member of the board of trustees of Occidental College, a director of the Children's Hospital of Los Angeles and a director and treasurer of the Hollywood Bowl Association.

In 1965, Herbert Hoover, Jr., president of the United Geophysical Co. from 1935–53, became Club president.

Several Club leaders were to retire or die during the 1960s. Harry Bauer died in 1960 after serving twenty-nine years as president, the longest in Club history. Edward Valentine resigned in 1965 as a director for reasons of ill health. In 1964 the Club's bylaws were amended to provide a more flexible number of directors: not less than nine nor more than twelve, with three of these permitted to reside outside Los Angeles County. Herbert Hoover, Jr., Milton Teague, past president of the California Chamber of Commerce and a director of Security First National Bank, and Dr. Arnold Beckman, chairman of the board of Beckman Instruments, Inc., became directors. General Counsel J. Allen Davis retired in 1959 and was replaced by Harry V. Cheshire, Jr. Joseph E. Havenner was named general manager in 1961 and in 1964 became executive vice president, succeeding Norman Thompson.

Club representatives participated actively in developing AAA policies on highway and motorist taxation, urban transportation, traffic operations, vehicle-operating problems, travel, motor-vehicle laws and law enforcement, administration, and national and civil defense. These long-term views and policies represent a concensus among the affiliated clubs of the AAA, but are not considered binding. While clubs generally adhere to these policies, they may follow divergent ones in their own areas if they so wish. By 1965, the AAA reported some 10 million members in the organization's various divisions and affiliated clubs throughout the U.S. and Canada.

The Interinsurance Exchange was, by now, a most successful institution, serving far more members of the Auto Club. Indeed, best insurance reports have consistently given it the highest possible ratings.

As the Exchange had grown, so had the complexity of highways. In 1958 the magazine "California Highways and Public Works" noted that there were already nearly 7½ million motor vehicles and predicted some 20 million Californians by 1970. It explained that the heavy emphasis on freeways was due to their proven ability to handle more traffic with more safety than any other type of road. For example, the average rate of fatalities during a selected number of years per 100 million vehicle miles was 2.62 on freeways and 9.37 on rural state highways. By the end of 1958, 467 miles of full freeway were to be completed, with an additional 215 miles under construction. Also, most of the 926 miles of expressway (with intersections at grade) had been designed for future conversion to freeway status. One year later the same magazine pointed out clearly what freeways had done to increase nearby land and property values, indicating that land prices had often multiplied five or ten times as a result of freeway completion. Gone was the old pattern of a highway becoming a breeding ground for commercial clutter which, in turn, defeated the original purpose of the highway.

In the late 1950s the State Highway Department, the leading senator on highway matters, Randolph Collier, and the motor clubs agreed that a more definite program and policy was needed for freeway development.

In 1957 Collier introduced Senate Concurrent Resolution 26 calling for the State Department of Public Works to undertake a study for an overall statewide freeway and express plan.

This led to the Freeway and Expressway Act of 1959. Supported by the motor clubs and other road groups, the act called for the construction of some 12,000 miles of freeways and expressways at a total cost of $10 billion within an estimated twenty years. The California freeway and expressway system incorporated the mileage of the Federal Interstate and Defense Highway System which Congress approved in 1956. The overall state system was geared to meet the projected demands of 1980, when there would be an estimated 31 million Californians with 17 million autos.

Financing was based on the assumption of a continued state gas tax of six cents per gallon, supplemental registration and other fees, the continued availability of federal assistance in building the Interstate System and other federal highways. Estimates indicated the cost and funds for the ambitious program would balance, although there was no provision for additional funds for city streets and county highways.

Meanwhile, a vast and constant debate swept legislative halls on these matters. Senator Collier in 1959 introduced Senate Concurrent Resolution 62 calling for a city street and county road study, outlining problems and deficiencies. A summary of demands for 1980 showed some $5 billion were needed for city streets and more than $7½ billion for county roads. In 1961 a bill was introduced which proposed a county levy of 1 percent of market value on vehicles in addition to the existing 2 percent of market value fee collected by the state. Both the Club and the California State Automobile Association opposed this bill. The legislature did not act, so the matter was postponed for two years, giving time for added study.

In 1963 the Collier-Unruh Local Transportation Act increased the gas tax from 6 to 7 cents per gallon, along with other motor-vehicle tax increases, and the money was to be spent by a complicated formula to meet city and county road deficiencies.

While the Club supported this increase to improve local roads, unfortunately this bill was amended at the last moment by a rider that the Club vigorously opposed. The rider authorized county boards of supervisors to levy local vehicle-license fees to subsidize rapid transit. It amounted to one-half of 1 percent of the market value of the vehicle, and the monies were to be used exclusively in rapid-transit development. In Los Angeles County, for example, the tax would be about $15 million a year for this purpose. The Club, while not opposed to mass transit, was against the idea of levying a tax on motor vehicles to subsidize it.

A second issue was also involved: duplication of a local property tax. Before 1935, motor vehicles were subject to both county and city personal-property taxes collected locally. But some assessors held that there was a loss of motor-vehicle tax through address changes or the like, and a law was passed requiring a certificate from local tax assessors before an auto registration could be renewed or transferred. It was a controversial bit of legislation that put a burden on many people.

In 1935 the state, with the support of the motor clubs, levied a vehicle-

PLATES *102 and 103 Though few are aware of the fact, traffic congestion was more severe in the thirties and forties than after the advent of the freeway system. Here, a shot of Alvarado at Wilshire Boulevard in 1937 contrasts strongly with a present-day shot of the four-level interchange in the Los Angeles civic center.*

license tax fee to insure payment of what amounted to a property tax on autos at the rate of 1¾ percent of actual market value, which was considered to be equal to the tax levied on other types of property. It was felt that this act allowed no escape and the state would be paid back for costs of collection. An appropriation was made to pay installments on state highway bonds from 1909, 1915 and 1919 with plans for the balance to be returned to counties and cities. The rate in 1948 was increased to 2 percent of actual market value. Hence, motorists had every reason to protest added attempts to allow local authorities to collect duplicate taxes on auto licenses by what was really another personal-property tax.

Between 1958 and 1965 there was a great deal of legislation affecting

autos and drivers, including a revised Motor Vehicle Code. In 1959 a maximum 65-mph speed limit was established. In 1961 the State Highway Transportation Agency was created, and in 1963 the Vehicle Code was amended again to allow California to cooperate with other states in exchanging information on serious traffic accidents. In 1963 the sales and use tax was applied to the sale of an auto by one owner to another. In 1965 registration fees were increased from $8 to a total of $11 by 1968 to enlarge the California Highway Patrol.

A continuing and paramount concern of the Club was smog. The yellowish, stinging pall which had first become an issue in 1945 became more harassing as the years passed. The Club had been deeply involved in the search for a solution, assigning staff engineers to observe and assist officials involved in air pollution research. A variety of steps had been taken by local authorities. An Air Pollution District had been established in 1947, a program of smog alerts put into effect in 1955, incinerators outlawed in 1957, high-sulphur-content fuel for industry made illegal in 1959.

Yet something more had to be done. Air Pollution had not disappeared. In fact, it had spread and was now of concern to many portions of the state. In 1959 the State Legislature ordered the State Department of Public Health to establish standards for the quality of ambient air and set quantitative limits on the various pollutants emitted by an automobile in operation.

The following year, at a special session, the legislature created the State Motor Vehicle Pollution Control Board and charged it with controlling contaminants within the limits set down by the State Department of Public Health. The stated goal was to bring back the quality of 1940 air by 1970. The Club lent its facilities and talent to the effort, participating in a test of 1,000 automobiles at Club headquarters. (One result of the test was a lowering in the estimate of average vehicle hydrocarbon emissions from 1,300 parts per million to 900 parts per million.)

While the Club advocated all reasonable steps in the anti-smog fight, it opposed some "remedies" which seemed hysterical, unproved or excessive. Typical was a proposal to require annual inspection of the crankcase device, which first appeared on 1961 models sold in California. While the devices had proved effective in reducing some 30 percent of the hydrocarbons emitted by autos, the Club questioned the need for a costly compulsory check of so simple a device.

The Club followed a similar policy regarding the more complicated (and important) exhaust control device. While endorsing the need for such devices, the Club cautioned that they be tested adequately and be reasonably priced, before requiring motorists to acquire them.

By 1965, Senate Bill 317 required that all 1966 or later motor vehicles be equipped with an exhaust and crankcase device, and factory installation of them on new autos to be sold in California was routine in the U.S. auto industry.

The Club's other departments were comparably busy during these bustling years. The adjustment and Traffic Department, for example, paid fines and forfeitures of nearly $3 million on 245,602 traffic citations for members and issued bail bonds in some cases. The Emergency Road Service in 1965 answered 1,230,000 calls for help by members. In three days alone during a November storm there were 45,000 emergency road-service calls. The ten dispatch offices of the Club had more than 1,000 service vehicles working around the clock during this hectic month.

The Public Safety Department conducted fifteen freeway driving clinics in 1965 and offered the new service of a portable speedometer testing device which checked 6,544 autos for owners. It turned special attention to the problem of bicycle safety, testing on school grounds 22,478 bicycles for brakes, wheel alignment and balance. Safety films were shown by Club staffers to a total audience of 522,811, and another 7,507 heard speeches on the subject.

The Touring Department supplied Club members with nearly 4 million folder maps, 1½ million travel guides and 7 million strip maps, as well as thousands of tour books. The World Travel Department aided some 75,000 members with tour and accommodations reservations in foreign lands. The License Department handled 903,000 motor-vehicle transactions during the same year.

For years the Club had been making driving-time studies in the Los Angeles area. The Engineering Department conducted annual time-and-distance studies on freeways and major arterial roads—particularly for information on changes in peak-hour driving experiences. The findings were illuminating, and dispelled the popular notion that traffic congestion is on the upswing in the Los Angeles metropolitan area. For example, average peak-hour travel speeds increased from 24 mph in 1957 to 31 mph in 1965, while during the same years auto registration in the area rose by 1.5 million. Club engineers attribute this dramatic development to the growing freeway system and improvements in many arterial streets. As the freeway moves closer to completion, it is anticipated that commuting speeds will reflect an even greater increase.

In one aspect of public service, the Club's participation has diminished rather than grown over the years. For decades the Club had performed the task of signing public streets and highways. But the phenomenal growth of California forced the Club to reluctantly give up its sign-posting duties; it could not absorb the mushrooming costs nor respond quickly enough to signing needs. Consequently, the Division of Highways and the Club agreed in 1947 that the Club would discontinue posting signs on state highways; in 1956 the Club also stopped sign placement on city streets.

Nevertheless, the Club's Sign Services Department continues in an advisory and cooperative capacity, recommending to the state and other signing agencies sound principles in numbering and naming highways and sign design. The Club is particularly interested in the standardization of signs so that the motorist is not confused when he moves from one jurisdiction to another.

The Engineering Department has taken on new tasks in recent years. One is to issue maps annually which show the status of the freeway system in the Los Angeles area. It is also continuing its long-time study (since 1920) of hazardous locations on streets and highways, with staff members investigating complaints, reporting the dangers to highway authorities, and often cooperating in the determination of remedial measures.

All such activities are consistent with the Club's primary objective: "To perpetuate and enhance the character of the Automobile Club as a not-for-profit service organization dedicated to the protection and best interests of the Club members, the motoring public, and the community."

As the Club moves from the present to the future, it is particularly mindful of a corollary purpose: to give maximum personal service to its members.

Chapter 18

TODAY AND THE FUTURE

"To perpetuate the Automobile Club of Southern California as a not-for-profit, non-stock organization serving its members by providing personal and convenient services that meet their motoring needs, and by maintaining a role of active leadership in those fields of public service that serve the best interests of the motoring public and the community."

—Philosophy and Objectives of the Automobile Club of Southern California.

As in our own personal lives, an organization lives year by year with its own dreams, drives and aspirations. Crises always seem to occupy the present. It looks toward the future with both concern and delight.

There have been flamboyant, happy, grim and colorful years for the Club since those ten young men met on the chilly night of December 13, 1900, to promote the idea of a club for owners of self-propelled motor vehicles. Since then a network of dirt roads, then great highways, and finally freeways have spread across southern California. The happy Sunday races spun off into history with changing times, as did the chugging cavalcades, the carefree explorations, the great struggles for legislation to aid the motorist.

Services and needs altered or disappeared with the roll of the decades —sign-posting, insurance, financing, tax woes. The grand tours and road-charting expeditions went over the horizon. The great Depression came and went, and then there were the desperate times of World War II. The Club had faced it all, weathered it all, and grew and prospered.

The present has brought its own changes and speculations. Today, the auto itself—root structure of the Club—continues to cost more and more. But then so does everything else.

The subtle and not-so-subtle pressures continue for new safety features, for changes in design, for new gadgets and luxuries.

In the final analysis, of course, it is the public which decides taste and design, while the manufacturers pursue market trends based on sales and surveys. But the trend is happily toward both the utilitarian and aesthetic. Comforts too numerous to total have been added. So has automatic shifting, power steering, power brakes, electronic aids—some of them devised decades ago. "Economy" is still another watchword as prices go up.

Ahead? One can only speculate. There is the distant prospect of autos which will be moved by electric power as a remedy for air pollution, but the near future is not likely to see a practical product on the market. Turbine engines are also being toyed with and discussed in some select automotive circles, but they seem as far in the future as the battery-operated vehicle. Beyond that, only a gleam in the eye of dreamers, is the atomic car.

All that aside, the tendency now seems to be to produce cars of every style, size and price to meet the needs of the U.S. market. Economy compacts, medium-priced compacts, station wagons, sedans with all kinds of optional equipment—the evolving panorama of auto offerings goes on and on.

Various theories come and go. Some engineers believe safety will be increased when autos are built not like wagons, from which they really evolved, but like bridges, with less stability and rigidity and more chances for expansion, so that the auto, not the human, will absorb the impact of a collision. Others stress more and more padding, safety glass and stronger structure. The dream of eliminating corrosion continues, with all manufacturers trying to find new secrets to combat moisture. Still others are happily turning and looking at the past for design, seeking ways to simplify the complicated mechanisms of today's steering, shifting and braking—without losing comfort and safety.

All these aspirations and speculations come under the scrutiny of the

PLATE *104 After moving from one small office to another, the Auto Club finally settled down in 1917 on Figueroa Street, about a mile from the present building.*

Club as it plans for the future. But the present, too, holds its own share of problems.

The Club set new growth records in 1967 to reach 921,915 members. It had seventy-two offices in the thirteen southern counties of California, three created during the year at Chula Vista, Arrowhead-Big Bear and El Cajon. Santa Paula also became a district office and personnel at Bishop, Pasadena and Inglewood moved into new and larger quarters. A sure sign of the historic role of the Club was found in the 50th anniversary celebrations at eight of the district offices.

The services the Club offered in 1967 would have bewildered the ten young men who had started the organization many decades before. Indeed, many would be incomprehensible to them. From an array of nearly 200 different maps and guides, some 5,790,000 individual maps were distributed, as well as 1,940,000 travel guides and tour books and 8,786,000 strip maps. All these aided the peripatetic southern Californians as they visited surfing and skiing areas, golf courses, beaches, campgrounds and parks and boating facilities. New maps and guides created during the year were for Death Valley, the Indian Country, the Palm Springs area and the northern half of Baja California.

World travelers—some 200,000 strong—sought Club aid, with 60,000 of them making travel arrangements through the World Travel Service, which offers help in such matters as reservations, tickets, group tours, cruises, driving permits, escorted tours, rental of autos in foreign lands and independent travel arrangements.

For those who wanted to "see America first," the Club's program of inspecting and approving accommodations, in conjunction with other AAA-affiliated clubs, aided more than 10 million people, with reporters inspecting and evaluating thousands of food and lodging establishments. Some 175,000 reservations were also made for members at approved hotels and motels. Meanwhile, the licensing department handled some 900,000 transactions, including 12,000 boat registrations.

Emergency Road Service, working twenty-four hours a day seven days a week from eighteen dispatching facilities, answered 1,535,074 calls for aid, with 290 contract stations utilizing more than 1,150 service trucks (most equipped with two-way radios). Too, a pioneer concept—the first of its kind anywhere—was initiated. Called the Tow Truck Driver Training program, its purpose is to train men for, and upgrade the quality of, assistance at the contract stations.

The Service Patrol was also busy in 1967, not only traveling more than 570,000 miles to aid motorists stalled on roads, but providing a variety of services at 137 fairs, parades and special events. Club personnel also conducted some 27,407 speedometer tests.

Quick credit approval and auto financing were improved by the Finance Department with a new computer system which allows same-day new-car finance service. The maximum contract was extended to thirty-six months and some 9,000 members took advantage of the Club's personalized, low-cost, new-car financing.

The Interinsurance Exchange continued to be southern California's leading insurer of private autos and issued 562,000 policies covering more than 700,000 cars during 1967. A total of $13,000,000 in policy-holder's dividends was issued.

The Highway Engineering Department was deeply immersed in such problems as public transportation and the need for a flexible transportation system. A staff post of transportation planning engineer was created during 1967, and the Traffic Management Study started in 1966 was completed early in 1967. The latter dealt with such concerns as traffic investigations in various cities and counties, including twelve speed zoning studies and the examination of some 660 hazardous traffic locations. Another study, of peak-hour freeway congestion in the Los Angeles area and the related problem of traffic advisory broadcasts, revealed that improvement was needed. Finally, the Club aided the Division of Highways in studying the Hollywood Freeway Ramp Closure Project. Studies were also made on freeway signing and on such related hardware as guardrails and guideposts.

Public safety education remained a vital concern, with fourteen freeway driving clinics, two power boat courses and eight car care courses being offered. The mobile speedometer testing unit visited fifty-five communities and tested 11,300 cars, while Public Safety Department consultants attended 1,846 meetings, had 7,087 film showings and made 1,041 school visits. Nearly 20,000 bicycles were tested at school grounds, nearly 3,500,000 safety booklets and posters were distributed and 549 dual control autos were provided to high schools in cooperation with new car dealers. A "first" was a motorcycle safety program in La Mirada that should serve as a model for many schools.

Automotive Engineering had two programs under way as a result of the advent of exhaust control devices on 1966 autos. First was a study to determine what emission levels could be expected from a random sampling of the newer autos; the second was to determine what effect maintenance had on the deterioration in efficiency of those exhaust control systems. More than 1,174 tests were made on members' cars and—in 1967— the maintenance evaluation program was expanded from a fleet of fifty to one hundred autos as part of a research contract with the state. It involved 800 tests to determine: the effect of maintenance on engines with mileage accumulation; what relationships there are between the emissions of a cold engine and one which has been run before testing; a comparative study of auto manufacturers' changes in exhaust control systems.

Air pollution has long been a subject of close study by the Club. The organization first became involved after World War II, although many then felt the auto was being unfairly accused. "I went later to the General Motors testing lab in Detroit and visited their smog chamber," recalls Joseph E. Havenner, executive vice president, "and I smelled Los Angeles there." But many questions remain. Will present methods of tuning cars really have any effect on the emission of pollutants? Can some simple test be found to determine when an auto is in violation of smog control laws? The Club's past concern with air pollution and the Club's increasing role in research studies led to the opening in 1967 of a new air pollution laboratory to fulfill a state contract.

Auto safety and accident investigations were still other facets of the work done by the Club's automotive engineering staff, with special attention given wheel failure due to a manufacturing defect. The Club's study of this led to a new testing program by the company involved. A Club investigation of a rash of auto fires also led to the conclusion that one particular brand of carburetor was the villain. The manufacturer was notified.

As usual, legislation affecting the auto owner and driver filled the hoppers in Sacramento. Taxes and auto operating costs were vital issues. One law passed in 1967, for example, raised minimum financial responsibility limits for personal injury from $10,000 and $20,000 to $15,000 and $30,000 on July 1, 1968. Other bills which concerned the Club would have raised taxes on motor vehicles and increased operating costs to subsidize rail transit, while still another called for a hike in license fee from the present 2 percent of market value to 2½ percent.

This 25 percent increase would have gone to the state and counties. It, like a bill calling for state and local sales tax on gasoline, was not passed. Other new laws in 1967 established a safety program to conform with federal standards, set limits on motor vehicle noise and strengthened smog control laws by establishing a new State Air Resources Board.

The demands of growth were as much with the Club as ever before. A study was under way to determine future computer needs. Plans were being made for new district offices. A survey showed the Club could take pride in employee morale. More than 39 percent of the Club's 4,031 employees had five or more years service, 229 had more than twenty years and forty-eight had more than thirty.

Finally, WESTWAYS' circulation increased during 1967 from 406,648 to 456,187. Growth in pages was steady, and one particular issue devoted to the California Gold Rush soon became a collector's item. A number of awards were received for the magazine's artwork and editorial content —including an Award of Merit from the American Association for State and Local History.

The *Auto Club News Pictorial* increased its circulation from 800,000 to 871,000 in 1967. The Public Relations Department also continued its program of publishing various materials, producing films, tapes and records for radio and television.

But even as the Club grows, it must look to the future.

The whole elaborate problem of freeway financing dominates much of highway discussion today. Roughly 40 percent of California's freeways are in the southern part of California. There may be partisan battles along geographical lines to change this ratio. Inflation and high costs have become factors to reckon with since the freeway program was first outlined. The complicated debate over rapid transit is still another serious matter. The Club's stand is that special taxes levied on the basis of highway use should be devoted solely to highway improvements. Highway construction is vital to the future welfare of the state, and any diversion of highway funds to non-highway purposes would be detrimental not only to the motorist but to the entire California economy.

The original freeway system was planned with the idea that inflation would be a factor to reckon with in the future. Even so, inflation and the resultant cost increases have outrun expectations, and the cost of the 12,500-mile system will exceed the original estimate of $12 billion.

Today, there are more than 2,500 miles of freeway, some 600 miles of multi-laned divided expressways, and approximately 900 miles of two-lane expressways in operation. Much remains to be done if California is to get the transportation system she needs.

Today the Club's board of directors includes the most distinguished civic, business and professional leaders of southern California. Lloyd L. Austin, chairman of the board of Security First National Bank, served as president of the Club from 1963 to 1965. A director of the Club since 1956, Austin is also a director of the Carnation Co., Northrop Corp. and the California State Chamber of Commerce. He's a trustee of Occidental College, a director and treasurer of the Hollywood Bowl Association and on the Board of Councilors for the Graduate School of Business Administration at USC in addition to an array of other roles in civic life.

Dr. Arnold O. Beckman, a distinguished scientist, became a member of the board in 1965. A resident of Orange County, he is the chief executive officer and chairman of the board of Beckman Instruments, Inc., manufacturers of electronic instrumentation, a firm which he founded in 1935. A former member of the chemistry faculty at Caltech, he serves on the institution's board of trustees and was elected board chairman in 1964 and is also on the advisory board of California State College at Fullerton. He serves as a trustee of the California Museum Foundation. He is also a director of the Security First National Bank, the Southern California Edison Co., Continental Airlines, the California State Chamber of Commerce, Stanford Research Institute and a trustee of System Development Corporation.

Asa V. Call, chairman of the executive committee of the Pacific Mutual Life Insurance Co., has served as a Club director since 1946, and is currently president, succeeding Herbert Hoover, Jr. A longtime Los Angeles civic leader, Call has held important roles with such organizations as the California Cement Co., California Bank, Gladding McBean Co., Pacific Am. Investors and Founders Fire and Marine Insurance Co. He is also a member of both the California Bar Association and American Bar Association.

Knox Farrand, a member of the board since 1949, of the Los Angeles law firm, Farrand, Fisher and Farrand, is, in addition to being a member of the California Bar Association and the American Bar Association, a former trustee of the Los Angeles County Bar Association, a member of the board of directors of the Welfare Federation and a past trustee of the Claremont Men's College.

Herbert Hoover, Jr., consulting engineer and son of the late president, first joined the board in 1960. President of the Club in 1965–66, he has a long list of distinguished roles. A former member of the research staff of Harvard Business School and teaching fellow at Caltech, he became president of the United Geophysical Co. in 1935 and chairman of the board in 1952. He is also a former president of the Consolidated Engineering Corp. and a former consultant to the governments of Venezuela, Iran and Peru. A special adviser to the U. S. Secretary of State and Under Secretary of State from 1954 to 1957, he is also a trustee of USC, Claremont Men's College and a director of Southern California Edison Co.

Frank L. King, also a past president (from 1961 to 1963), is the chairman of the board of Western Bancorporation and United California Bank. In addition, he is vice chairman of the board of trustees and treasurer of USC, a director of First Western Bank and Trust Co., Litton Industries, Pacific Indemnity Co., Pacific Mutual Life Insurance Co. and the Times-Mirror Co. He is also vice president and director of the Association of Registered Bank Holding Companies.

Director Thomas L. Lowe, president of the Newhall Land and Farming Co., is former executive vice president in charge of investments for the Pacific Mutual Life Insurance Co., a director of the Los Angeles Chamber of Commerce, California Taxpayers Association, and the All Year Club, as well as a trustee of Claremont Men's College and an elder of the Presbyterian Church.

Neil Petree, chairman of the executive committee of Barker Brothers Corp., first became a director in 1938. He is also a director of Bank of America, Gladding McBean, and the California State Chamber of Commerce. In addition, he is president of the Los Angeles Convention and Exhibition Center Authority and a member of the Governor's Traffic and Transportation Committee.

Milton Teague of Santa Paula, president of the Limoneira Co. and Limco Del Mar of Santa Paula, is a director of a vast array of business enterprises including Security First National Bank. He is president and director of Sunkist Growers, a past president of the Agricultural Council of California and the California State Chamber of Commerce.

Two outstanding community leaders retired from the board in 1968. They are Stuart O'Melveny, a director of Title Insurance and Trust, State Mutual Building and Loan Association, Southern California Gas Co., and Consolidated Steel Co., who had been a director of the Club since 1939, and Claiborn A. Saint, vice president of R. A. Rowan and Co., who became a Club director in 1947. Mr. Saint is also a former director of the Central City Association of Los Angeles, a past president of the Los Angeles Realty Board, a director of the Merchants and Manufacturers Association, the National Safety Council, and the Children's Hospital Society of Los Angeles.

Replacing O'Melveny and Saint on the Club's Board of Directors in 1968 were Terrell C. Drinkwater and T. M. McDaniel, Jr. Mr. Drinkwater is president and director of Western Air Lines, Inc., as well as being a director of Southern California Edison Co., Union Bank of Los Angeles, and Pacific Mutual Life Insurance Co. He has also been president and vice president of the Los Angeles Chamber of Commerce, a director of the Transportation Association of America, and a trustee of Pomona College.

T. M. McDaniel, Jr., was elected president of Southern California Edison Co. in 1968, the same year he joined the Club's board. A director and former executive vice president of Southern California Edison Co., Mr. McDaniel is also a director of the American Mutual Fund and the Kern County Land Co. In addition, McDaniel is a director of the Los Angeles Chamber of Commerce, the Los Angeles Better Business Bureau, and the Southern California Industry-Education Council.

If the board is rich with experience and honors, so too are today's executive personnel at the Club.

Joseph E. Havenner, named general manager in 1961, became the Club's executive vice president in 1964. He first joined the Club in 1941 as a traffic engineer. After returning from World War II, serving the Navy's Civil Engineering Corps at Guadalcanal, he managed the Public Safety Department for ten years and was appointed director of the Club's Engineering and Technical Services in 1956.

He is chairman of the Highway Committee of the AAA, a member of its Executive Committee, and a former member of the California Motor Vehicle Pollution Control Board, in addition to guiding the workaday affairs of the Club. Quite to be expected, he has served on a vast array of national, state, county and city boards and groups involved with engineering, highway and traffic problems.

Harry V. Cheshire, Jr., vice president and general counsel, joined the staff as associate counsel in 1952, became general counsel in 1959 and vice president in 1964. He has held the position of legislative counsel, as well as filling posts with the National Committee of Uniform Traffic Laws and Ordinances, the California Advisory Committee on Motor Vehicle Legislation and the Statewide Highway Committee of the California State Chamber of Commerce. He is also a director of the AAA and a member of its policy committee. In his legislative role he helped prepare the Citizen's Advisory Committee report on city and county road deficiencies and the financing study which followed.

Ralph L. Inglis, vice president for insurance at the Club, joined the Club in 1956 after having been vice president of both the Associated Indemnity Corporation in New York City and the American Association Insurance Group in St. Louis. He has been president of the board of the Founders' Insurance Co., president of the Western Insurance Information Service, director of the Pacific Insurance and Surety Conference and, today, serves on the board of governors of the Pacific Coast Insurance Advisory Association.

Lawrence J. Desmond, director of administrative services, joined the Club in 1960 as controller, after having been comptroller of Union Automobile Association in Bloomington, Illinois. He is an attorney and CPA.

Highway Engineer John W. McDonald, director of the Engineering and Technical Services Division, came to the Club in 1956 after working with the U. S. Bureau of Public Roads and the State Division of Highways.

Richard U. Robison, director of the Club's Legal Division, was formerly an attorney with the Union Oil Co. He is a member of the American Bar Association and has been the Club's legislative counsel in Sacramento, where he serves on a number of important legislative committees.

Thomas M. Smith, director of the Travel Services Division, started as a travel counselor with the AAA in Washington, D.C. He moved through various departments of the organization and was manager of the travel services department at AAA headquarters by 1949. In 1956 he came to the Club as manager of the Touring, Map Drafting and License

Department and in 1957 was appointed director of the Travel Services Division. Today, he is also vice president of the AAA National Touring Bureau and a member of the AAA World Travel Advisory Committee.

Cloid W. Farley, who joined the Club in 1941, is today director of the Field Operations Division. Previously he served as zone manager and before that as manager of the Hollywood, East Los Angeles and Bellflower offices.

Harold H. Dixon, director of the Insurance Underwriting Division, joined the Club in 1927. In the 1930s he was office supervisor in Glendale and became district manager in Burbank in 1946. After World War II he was promoted to the field secretary's office and in 1950 became manager of the Insurance Underwriting Department and was made director in 1961.

Attorney Claybourne H. King is the Club's secretary and joined the Club in 1957 after private practice.

With such seasoned personnel, it seems likely that the Club can face the future without trepidation. And what—as we can see now—is that future?

A military man, Lieutenant General James Harbord, U. S. Army, once observed: "The roads we travel so briskly lead out of dim antiquity, and you study the past chiefly because of its bearing on the living present and its promise for the future."

The auto itself has become more than a means of transportation. It is the product of free enterprise, a major factor in the U.S. economy and—for the individual—a symbol of freedom and a reward for effort and work. All projections indicate an ever-swelling increase in autos in the years to come. It will continue to be the No. 2 market demand, following only housing. More and more people will continue to live in urban areas in the years ahead, we can be certain. With this will come an unrelenting demand for the freedom of mobility which the auto provides.

Some planners claim the poor, for example, should not aspire to own an auto for recreation or to travel increased distances for work. But they do—and will. Rapid transit will not answer this yearning and demand. Some architects, too, look at urban sprawl and see the auto as an obstacle to planned urban neatness. At the Seattle World's Fair a few years ago one exhibit was a starry-eyed vision of the future city. It was disease-free, sterile, air-conditioned under a glass dome and with fixed transportation scurrying about to fixed destinations from fixed points.

Superficially, one could look at it as a problem-free, happy world of the future. Yet, it was—upon study—a direct violation of our ideals and freedoms. It was a symbol which was in strict conflict with a free society, a frightening dream of reorganization with no concern for human desires or self-determined needs.

There is a visible trend today from which certain safe predictions can be made. The southern California of the future will have a low population density and continue to spread. While there are those who contend that we should not extend, the simple fact remains that we shall. At the same time, downtown Los Angeles—which has never reached its legal limits of land use—will continue to build as a city center.

The future indicates that there will be more and more federal legislation on motorist and highway matters. Such law-making today seems geared to protect man against himself; often it is muddled. The idea of convincing an owner with a cheap, small auto to put a padded panel on the dashboard, for example, dominates in legislative thinking over any effort to encourage him to buy a well-built auto which will protect him better. And, of course, as the population increases and becomes more urbanized, legislative control of the citizen by regulations will likewise increase.

Still another prediction is that there will be an increasing demand to "do something" about the whole field of auto insurance. It is probable that there will be a complete re-examination of this field, and the question of liability—whether the victim or society should be compensated—will be under study in legislative halls.

Already, the federal government has moved into areas which were previously those of the local and state authorities, and it is apparent that they will play an even greater role in safety matters in the years ahead. Washington, D.C., will also have more and more to say about drunken driving, the operation of federally subsidized highways, licensing. All this will touch on the philosophical question of individual mobility. People, no doubt, will continue to want to go where they want when they want.

The issue of how to best preserve and enhance the mobility of all of southern California will be the the subject of furious debate in the years ahead. Uniform traffic laws for the entire U.S. are probably in the offing. This may come about through voluntary action by the states, or, more likely, the federal government will compel the adoption of certain traffic rules in all states upon the penalty of withholding federal highway funds. Today, as part of this trend, there is a centralized computer in Sacramento where all traffic records go on file and information on any motorist can be obtained in a half hour. In the future, this will tie into a centralized computer in Washington, D.C.

The Club itself must, of course, not only reckon with these probable changes, but be able to predict them. A few years ago the board of directors, headed by Frank L. King, decided that there was not adequate evidence that the Club knew its future course. Staffers set to work in an elaborate reappraisal of objectives and services. Club membership was then growing at the rate of 35,000 to 40,000 a year. It had weathered the 1958 recession and had been forced to raise the dues. It was growing fast. But where was it headed?

The staff study restated objectives. The purpose, it was determined, was to grow in appropriate proportion to the population of the area the Club served. Meanwhile, a fresh look was taken at what services were needed and in what ratio. Many had to be expanded. The road service facilities, for example, were broadened with two-way radios, teletypes, twenty-four-hour service and added decentralization. The goal: to answer any call within twenty minutes.

In the process of reaffirming objectives, the Club's headquarters was reorganized and data processing systems were included which would take the Club through 1980. By that time it is expected that the Club will have doubled in size. It was decided that pure numerical growth, however, is not necessarily good in itself. The prime objective, as executive vice president Joseph E. Havenner has pointed out, is service. "We must grow and accept the necessity of growth, but at the same time increase convenient, personalized service," he explained.

A market study a few years back also indicated that the Club's public image suffered from certain misconceptions. It was found that a large segment of southern Californians thought Club membership costed far more than it did, was unacquainted with Club services, and did not know it was affiliated with the AAA. A campaign to properly inform the public was undertaken.

With service as the primary objective, it was clear that the organization had to face mounting costs. On January 1, 1968, dues for first-year members were raised from $20 to $30, a fact which was expected to limit growth somewhat. "We are not seeking growth for growth's sake," Havenner explained. "We offer a quality product which is priced accordingly."

A variety of lesser decisions were made. The question of whether to move the Club headquarters to a more fashionable area was considered. A study showed that a rebirth of the area it occupies seems likely, and it was decided to stay in the old structure, adding 150,000 square feet in the same Spanish California design.

The essence of Club purpose remains service to members. "As we

PLATE *105   The Club moved into its present headquarters at Adams and Figueroa in 1923. Its Spanish motif was retained in subsequent additions to the structure and will be echoed in a planned future addition. Instead of one office, as in 1923, the Club now has a main office and seventy-two branch offices, and its membership has grown from 55 in 1903 to 921,915 in 1967.*

look ahead the name of the game is change," says Executive Vice President Havenner. "Changing requirements of the driver and auto owner. He is seeing his world shrink and his possibilities expand. He will take a plane to Yellowstone, for example, and then rent an auto. The Club must be ready to fill his needs.

"The need for maps has changed radically. There was a time not long ago when many people didn't need them all that much. Now, with freeways, that need is there again. Nothing is static."

Similarly, the complicated problem of transportation in general changes constantly. "The day is long past when the auto shaped the city," Havenner explains. "We must find a transportation system which will serve the needs of people most efficiently. We must envision transportation concepts for the year 2000, and not resort to the concepts of 1900!"

The future always brings with it issues and crises not foreseen. Organizations—as well as people—must be flexible and rational in facing them, for any organization is, in the last analysis, only people. In the past, the Club drew strength from having had the men—both as directors and staff—with the capacity to meet any challenge. The future? There is no reason to believe that capacity will be any less, nor the achievements less significant.